A Complete Reference to
to
SAP
Material Management

Acknowledgments

I would like to dedicate this book to my family & friends because what I am today is due to their teachings and blessings, and to my wife Sunita & my daughter for all their support and encouragement whithout which I could have never complete this book.

I would also like to acknowledge the help and support received from my colleagues during writing of this book. The opportunity to work on challenging projects over the years has helped me hone my technical skills and enabled to write this book.

Special thanks to Mr. Brijesh Prajapati and Mr. Nishant Choubey for their support and encouragement.

.........................Rajesh Vyas

INDEX

SAP R/3

E Enterprise
R Resource
P Planning

S System
A Application
P Product in data processing
R Real time
3 Tier Architecture

System (GUI /PS): SAP GUI interacts with an application server using SAP present at protocol. It is an interface between the user and application server.

Application server: SAP Application is written ABAP/4 (Advanced business application program language 4th generation) and is identified by system instance number (00 – 99)

Data base server: A remote SQL protocol is used for the data transfer
It maintains the collection of tables and the relationship, through open SQL or native SQL all records will be updated.
SAP R/3 system was identified by SID (System identification number)

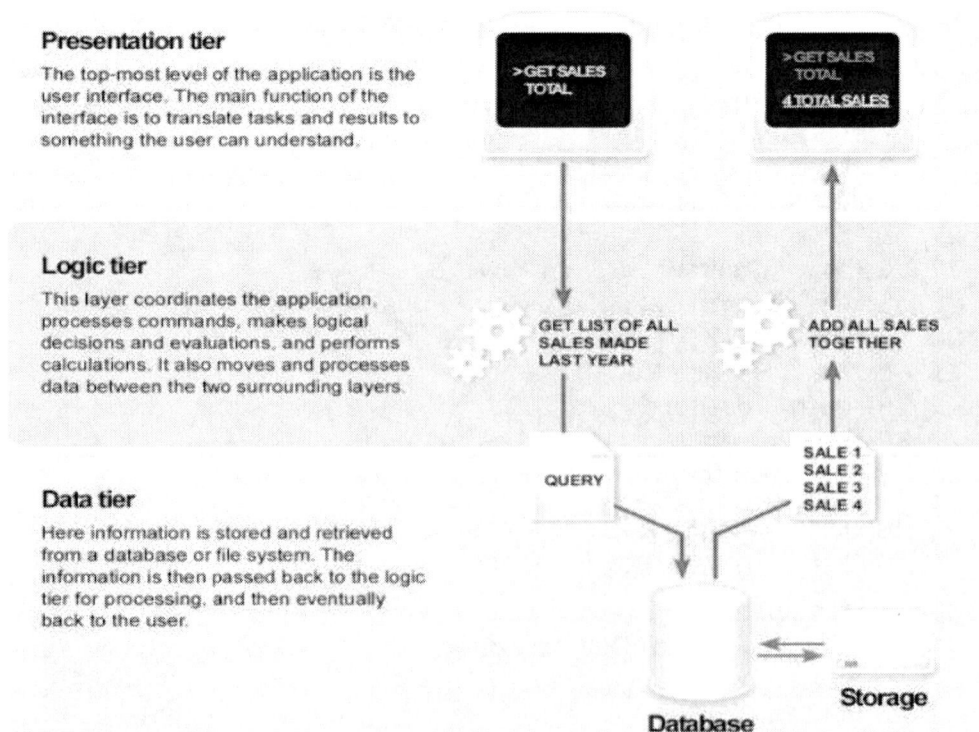

Presentation tier

The top-most level of the application is the user interface. The main function of the interface is to translate tasks and results to something the user can understand.

> GET SALES
TOTAL

> GET SALES
TOTAL
4 TOTAL SALES

Logic tier

This layer coordinates the application, processes commands, makes logical decisions and evaluations, and performs calculations. It also moves and processes data between the two surrounding layers.

GET LIST OF ALL
SALES MADE
LAST YEAR

ADD ALL SALES
TOGETHER

Data tier

Here information is stored and retrieved from a database or file system. The information is then passed back to the logic tier for processing, and then eventually back to the user.

QUERY

SALE 1
SALE 2
SALE 3
SALE 4

Database

Storage

Processing a user Request

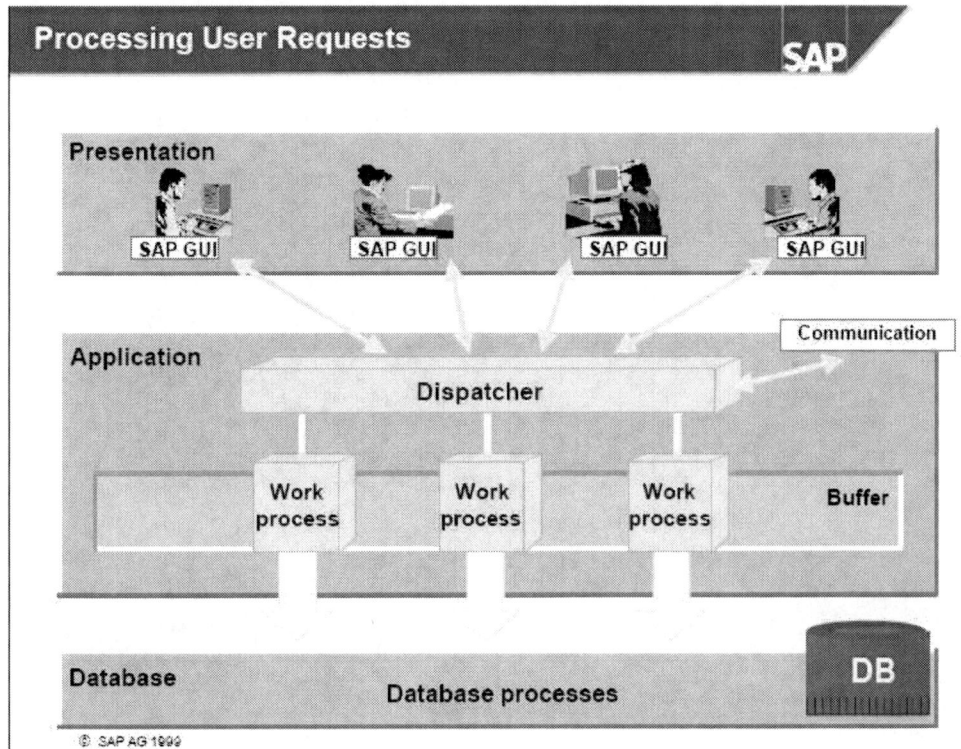

The central process in the R/3 application layer is the dispatcher. Together with the operating system, the dispatcher controls the resources for the R/3 applications. The main tasks of the dispatcher include distributing transaction load to the work processes, connecting to the presentation layer, and organizing communication.

In User screen the SAP presentation program SAP GUI receives input, converted into its own format, and then sent to the dispatcher. The processing requests are then saved by the dispatcher in request queues and processed according to "first in / first out".

In The dispatcher distributes (dispatches) the requests one after the other to the available work processes. Data is actually processed in the work process. The user that sent the request through the SAP GUI is usually not assigned the same work process, because there is no fixed assignment of work processes to users.

Once the data has been processed, the processing result from the work process is sent through the dispatcher back to the SAP GUI. The SAP GUI interprets this data and generates the output screen for the user with the help of the operating system on the front-end computer.

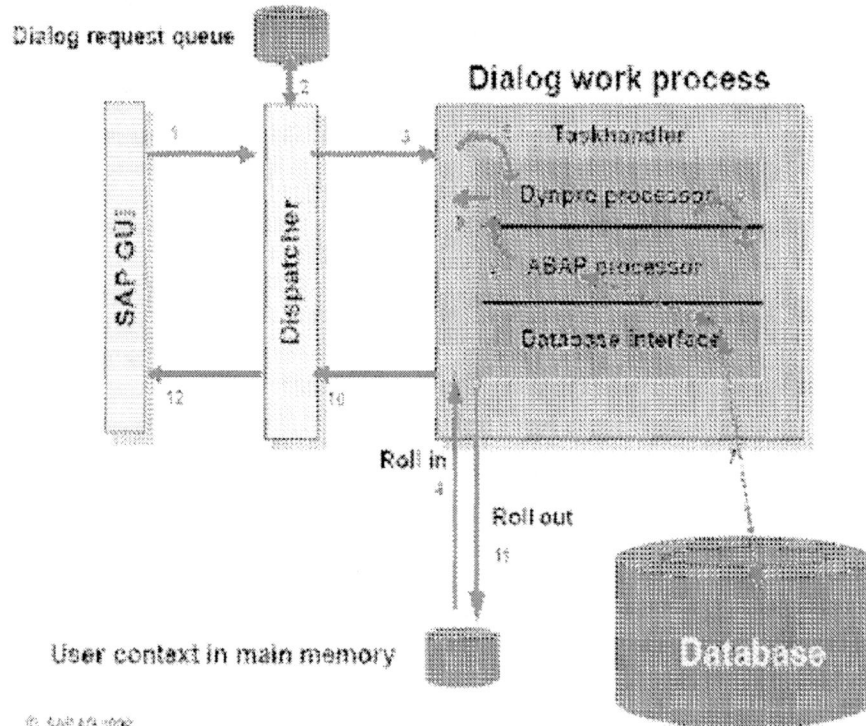

Dialog request queue

Dialog work process

Taskhandler

Dynpro processor

ABAP processor

Database interface

SAP GUI

Dispatcher

Roll in

Roll out

User context in main memory

Database

© SAP AG 1999

Client: It is a logical unit or independent unit, which is used for to organize a specific organization data.

There are 3 types of clients
- 000 client which is developed by SAP
- 001 to 999 It is reference client
- 066 Early watch server client

SYSTEM LANDSCAPE

The system landscape contains all the SAP Systems that you have installed. It can consist of several system groups, who's SAP Systems are linked by transport routes.

After you decide which clients you need and which roles you want them to have, you need to decide how to distribute them amongst the different SAP Systems. You can set up multiple clients independently of one another in a single SAP System. However, when you configure the data, you must remember that cross-client Customizing settings and Repository objects are identical for all clients in a single SAP System. Changes made in one client apply immediately to all clients in the system.

Three-System Landscape:
SAP recommends a three-system landscape in which each of the central clients has its own SAP System.

This consists of a development system DEV, a quality assurance system QAS and a production system PRD. The development system contains the Customizing client CUST, the quality assurance system contains the quality assurance client QTST and the production system contains the production client PROD. Make all changes to Customizing data and Repository objects in the Customizing client. When you release the corresponding change requests, they are transported into the quality assurance client. This means that changes to cross-client data only appear in the quality assurance client after the transport. In the quality assurance client you can test whether the transports are complete, or whether any linked changes are missing and are still in unreleased change requests. If the test is successful, the change requests are transported into the production client. The production client is completely separate from the other clients as regards cross-client data.

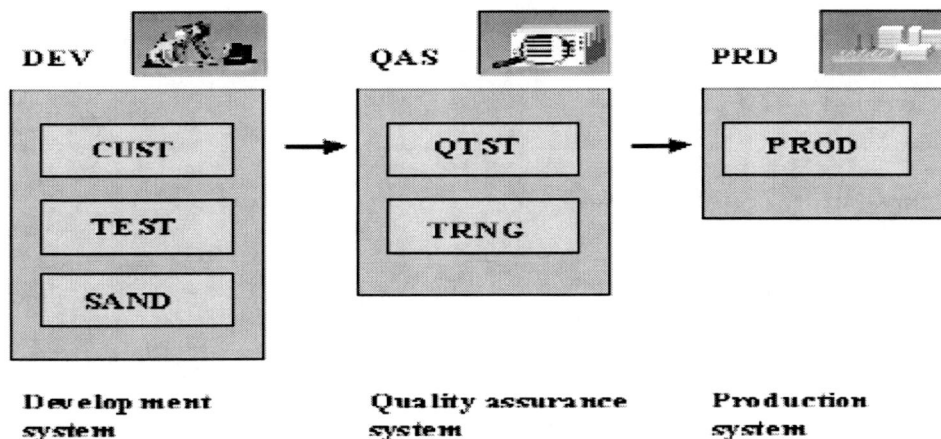

DEV	QAS	PRD
CUST	QTST	PROD
TEST	TRNG	
SAND		

| Development system | Quality assurance system | Production system |

ORGANIZATION STRUCTURE

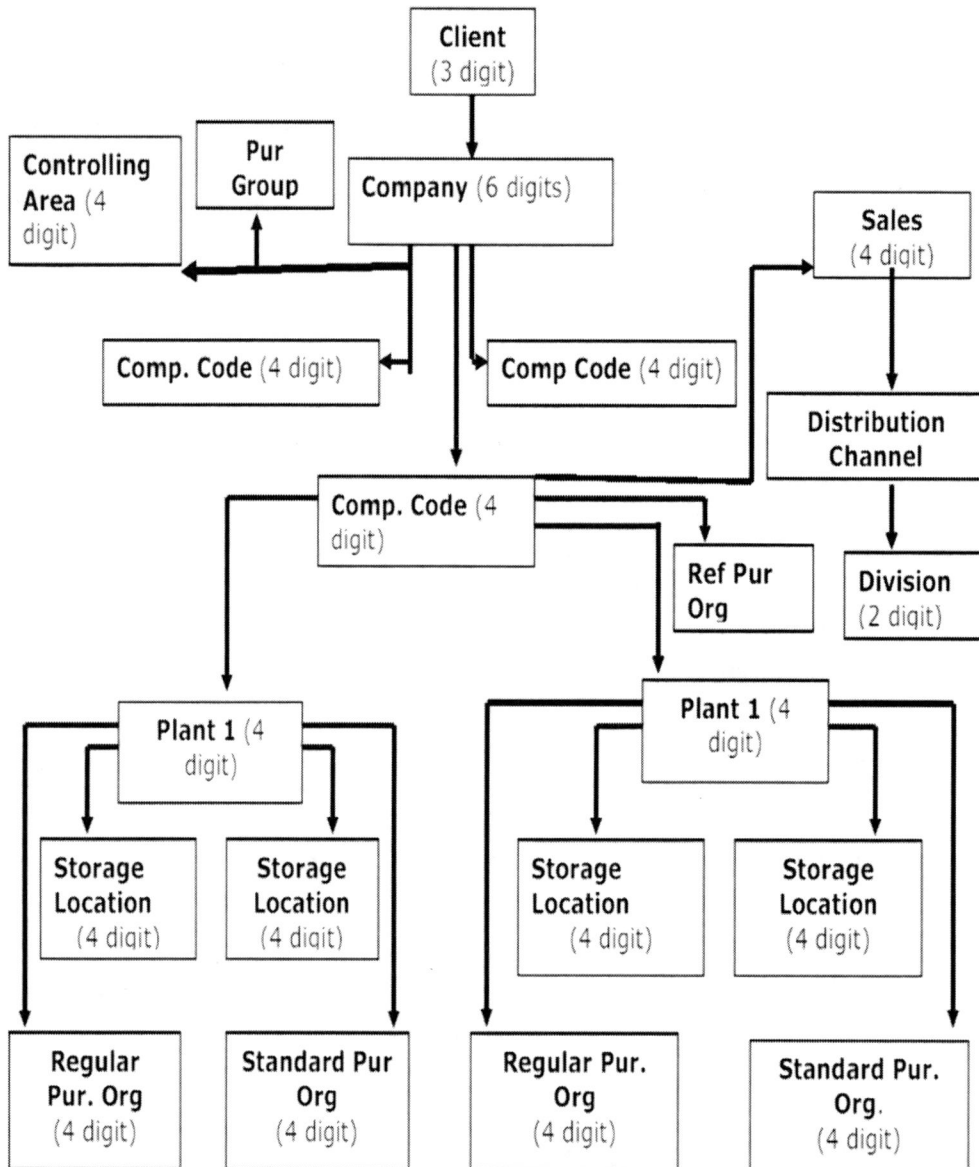

Note: - {1 Sales Org + 1 Distribution Channel + 1 Division = Sales Area}

Client: It is a logical unit or independent unit, which is used for to organize a specific organization data.

IMPLEMENTATION PROCESS

First we have to prepare documentation about the client business (like turnover, vendors, customers, payments, materials, production, marketing etc.)

The implementer company shall make two teams (1) Steering team (2) Steering community.

Steering team (SAP functional consultants) prepares a detailed documentation about the client with the help of core team (client company team) & this study is known as **Feasibility Study**. After that the steering team handed over this documentation to Steering community (Project manager, Sr. software engineer, and other higher authorities).

Steering community prepares the BBP (Business Blue Print). BBP Prepares in MS-Word

- **ASAP: -** Accelerated System Application Product in Data Processing.
- **Business Process: - ASAP Methodology**
  1. Project Preparation
  2. BBP (Business Blue Print)
  3. Realization
  4. Final Preparation
  5. Go live & Support

- **Project Preparation: -**
  It consists of identifying team members & development strategy as how to go.
  > AS – IS (Existing Process followed, requirements)
  > TO – BE (Requirement analysis and best process recommended)
  > Difference between (AS – IS) & (TO - BE) is called GAP Analysis.

- **Business Blue Print (BPP): -**
  It is a legal documentation between client & the company (implementer / service provider). We have to understand the current business process of client & analyzing the business & prepare documentation. It is a detailed documentation for the client.

- **Realization: -**
  This Phase is used to Implement or migrate the entire business of client from Non-SAP environment to SAP environment

- **Final Preparation: -**
  This phase is used for testing & end user training. After successfully completion of this phase client is ready to run business in SAP R/3.

- **Go live & Support: -**
  In this phase we deliver the project end date & end user training at client site.

- Client setup is done by **BASIS (Business Administration System Integrated Software)**. It is a logical unit or independent unit, which is used to organize a specific organization data

Company
Company Code   SAP FI/CO consultant
Controlling Area

- Sales Part is done by SAP SD consultant
  {1 Sales Org + 1 Distribution Channel + 1 Division = Sales Area}
- Rest is done by SAP MM consultant (Plant, Storage location, Pur Org., Ref Pur Org)

- **IDES**: - Internet Demonstration Evaluated System. (Complete SAP System used for educational purpose)

- **IMG**: - Implementation guide (Customizing purpose)

- Maximum number of screen or sessions can be opened is 6.

  Transaction Code: - **/N (T.Code)** → Closes the current session & opens the new session.
  Transaction Code: - **/O (T.Code)** → Minimizes the current screen & opens new session.

- **Difference between SAP 4.7 & ECC 5.0, ECC 6.0**
  ECC 5.0 & ECC 6.0 has its own database SAP DB, MAX DB

Path of SPRO

SAP EASY ACCESS → *TOOLS* → *CUSTOMIZING* → *IMG* →*SPRO*

CUSTOMIZE SETTINGS

Define Company: -

The organizational unit for which individual financial statements can be drawn up according to the relevant commercial law, all company codes within a company must use the same transaction chart of accounts and the same fiscal year breakdown. The company code currencies can be different.

SPRO → SAPIMG → Enterprise Structure → Definition → FI A/C → Define Company

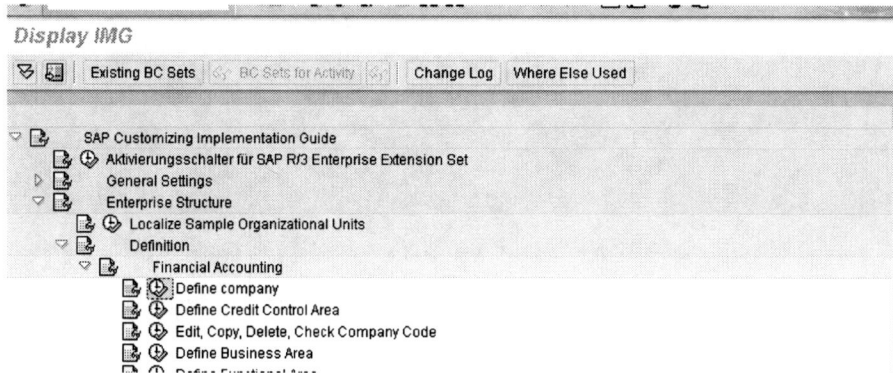

Click on New Entries

Company	Company name	Name of company 2	
1	Gesellschaft G00000		
2100	IDES Portugal		
2300	IDES España		
2600	IDES Luxemburg		
210000	IDES Portugal		
210099	IDES Portugal-Corp.Oth.Segment		
2100BA	IDES Portugal - B21 Rollup Co.		

Enter the Fields & Save

New Entries: Details of Add | Save (Ctrl+S)

Company	XYZ
Company name	XYZ
Name of company 2	XYZ

Detailed information

Street	ABCDEF
PO Box	12345
Postal code	000
City	
Country	IN
Language Key	EN
Currency	INR

Define Company Code: -

The smallest organizational unit for which a complete self-contained set of accounts can be drawn up for purposes of external reporting

SPRO → SAPIMG → ES → DEF → FI A/C → Edit, Copy, Delete, Check Company Code

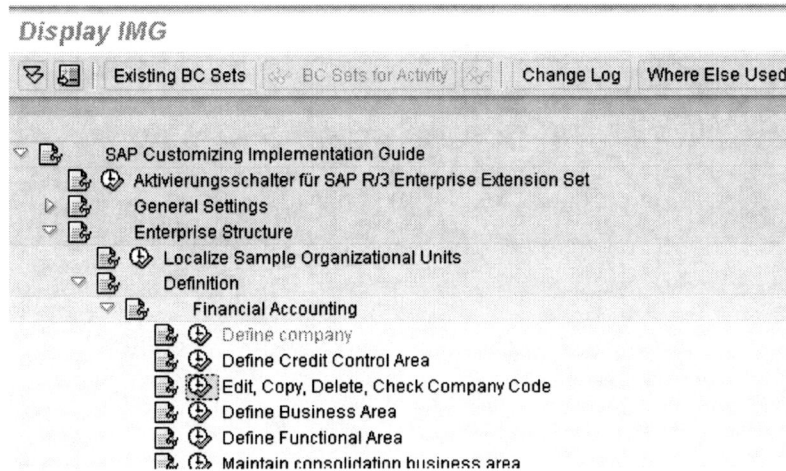

Display IMG

| | | Existing BC Sets | BC Sets for Activity | | Change Log | Where Else Used |

SAP Customizing Implementation Guide
    Aktivierungsschalter für SAP R/3 Enterprise Extension Set
    ▷ General Settings
    ▽ Enterprise Structure
        Localize Sample Organizational Units
        ▽ Definition
            ▽ Financial Accounting
                Define company
                Define Credit Control Area
                Edit, Copy, Delete, Check Company Code
                Define Business Area
                Define Functional Area
                Maintain consolidation business area

Double Click on Copy, Delete, Check Company Code

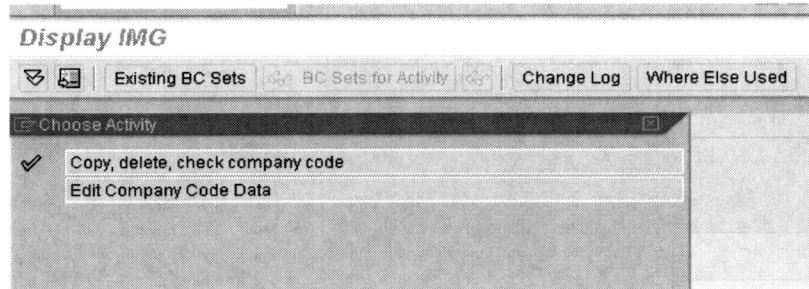

Display IMG

| | | Existing BC Sets | BC Sets for Activity | | Change Log | Where Else Used |

Choose Activity

✓   Copy, delete, check company code
      Edit Company Code Data

Click on Copy Button

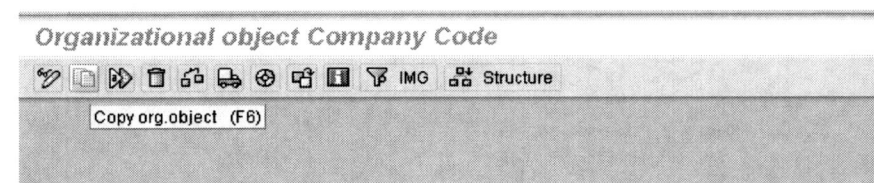

Organizational object Company Code

| | | | | | | | | | | IMG | Structure |

Copy org.object (F6)

Enter From Company Code & To Company Code

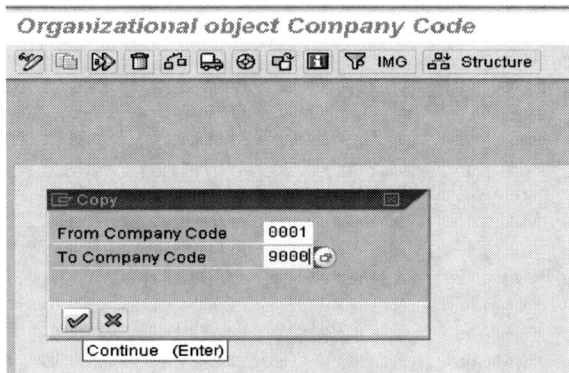

Organizational object Company Code

Copy

From Company Code   0001
To Company Code   9000

Continue (Enter)

Keep pressing Enter button until the from company code displays

After Defining Company Code go to **T. Code OMSY** to change the Fiscal Year & Month (If Material Master is created then go for **T. Code MMPV)**

Define Plant: -

An organizational unit serving to subdivide an enterprise according to production, procurement, maintenance, and materials planning aspects. It is a place where either Material are produced or goods and services provided

SPRO → SAPIMG → ES → DEF → Logistics General → Define, Copy, Delete Check Plant

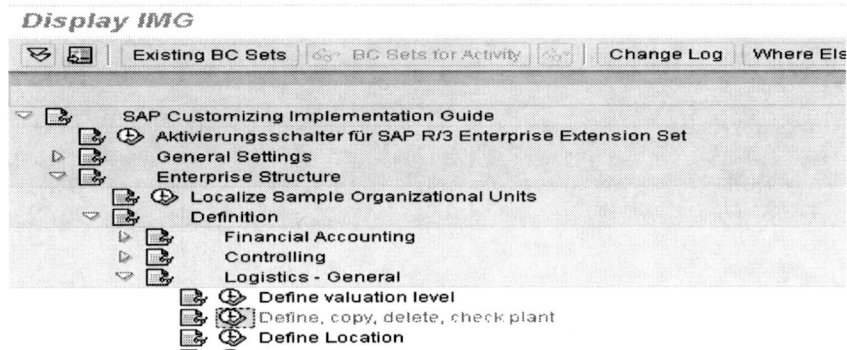

Display IMG

| | | Existing BC Sets | BC Sets for Activity | | Change Log | Where Els |

- SAP Customizing Implementation Guide
  - Aktivierungsschalter für SAP R/3 Enterprise Extension Set
  - General Settings
  - Enterprise Structure
    - Localize Sample Organizational Units
    - Definition
      - Financial Accounting
      - Controlling
      - Logistics - General
        - Define valuation level
        - Define, copy, delete, check plant
        - Define Location

Double Click on Define Plant

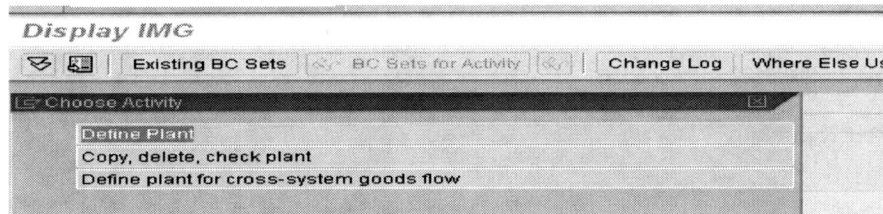

Display IMG

| | | Existing BC Sets | BC Sets for Activity | | Change Log | Where Else Us |

Choose Activity

Define Plant
Copy, delete, check plant
Define plant for cross-system goods flow

Click on New Entries

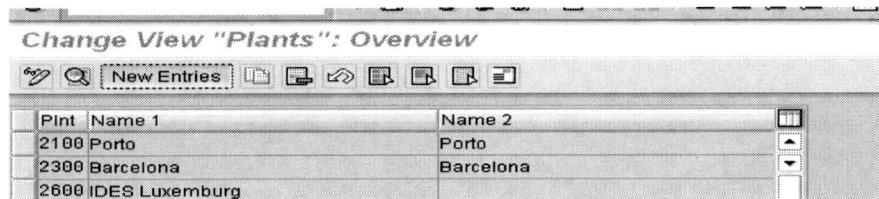

Change View "Plants": Overview

| | | New Entries | | | | | | | | |

Plnt	Name 1	Name 2	
2100	Porto	Porto	
2300	Barcelona	Barcelona	
2600	IDES Luxemburg		

Enter the Plant & Click on Address Button

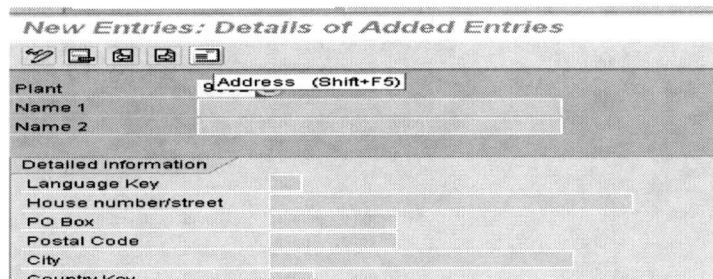

New Entries: Details of Added Entries

| | | | | |

Plant   Address (Shift+F5)
Name 1
Name 2

Detailed information
Language Key
House number/street
PO Box
Postal Code
City
Country Key

Enter the Fields (like Company Name, company address etc)

Edit address: 9002			
Name			
Title	Company		
Name	XYZ PLANT		
	XYZ PLANT		
Search terms			
Search term 1/2	XYZ PLANT		
Street address			
Street/House number			
Postal code/City	0000		
Country	IN India	Region	
Time zone	UTC+53		
PO box address			
PO Box	12345		
Postal Code	0000		
Company postal code			
Communication			
Language	English	Other communication...	
Telephone		Extension	
Fax		Extension	
E-Mail			

Change View "

Plant   90(
Name 1   !
Name 2   !

Detailed information
Language Key
House number/street
PO Box
Postal Code
City
Country Key
Region
County code
City code
Jurisdiction Code
Factory calendar

Note: Address d(
         The chang(

✓ ⊽ 🖨 Preview 🔓 🗗 International Versions ✖

Press Enter & Save it

Create / Maintain Storage Location: -

A storage location is the place where stock is physically kept within a plant. There may be one or more storage locations within a plant.

SPRO → SAPIMG → ES → DEF → Material Mgmt → Maintain Storage location

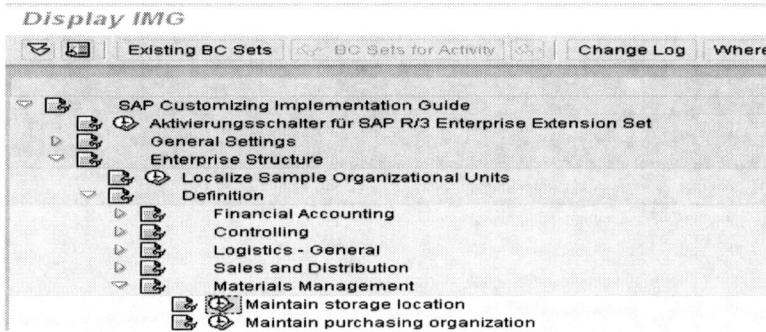

Enter the Plant Number & Press Enter

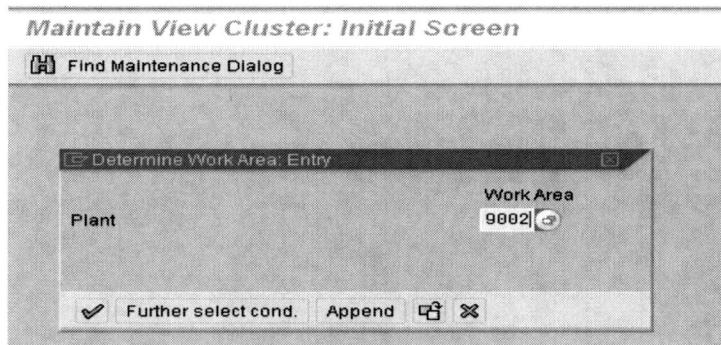

Click on New Entries

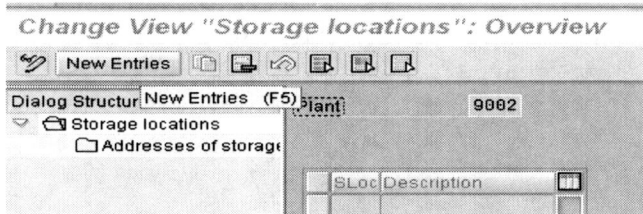

Enter Storage Location & Description & Save

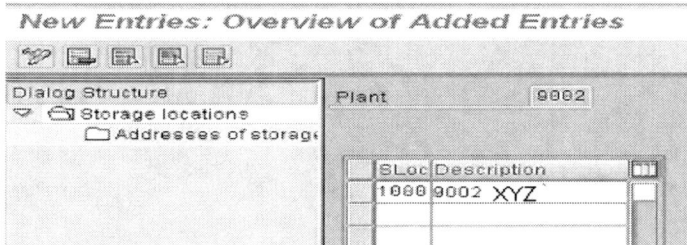

Create / Maintain Purchasing Organization: -

It procures materials and services, negotiates conditions of purchase with vendors, and is responsible for such transactions.

(Three types: plant specific, cross plant & cross company code)

SPRO → SAPIMG → ES → DEF →   Material Mgmt →Maintain Purchasing Org

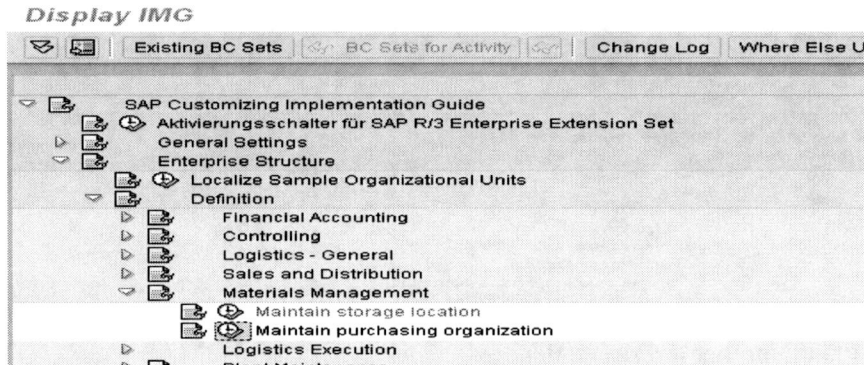

Click on New Entries

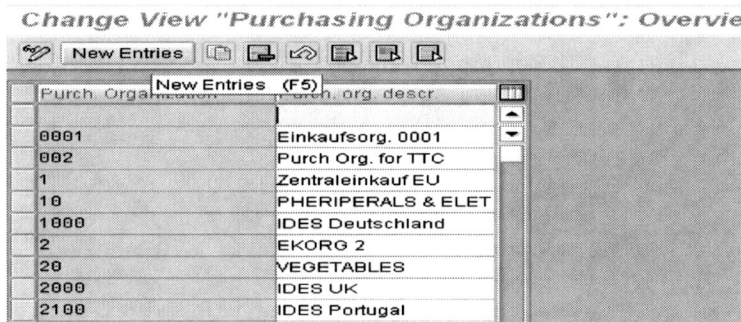

Enter the Purchasing Organization & Purchasing Org Description & Save

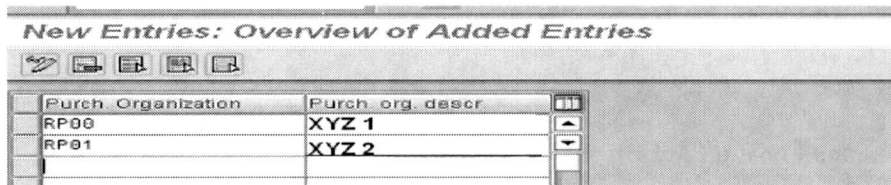

Create Purchasing group: -

It is a key of buyer or group of buyers, who is/are responsible for certain purchasing activities

SPRO → SAP IMG → MM →Purchasing → Vendor Master → Create Purchasing Group

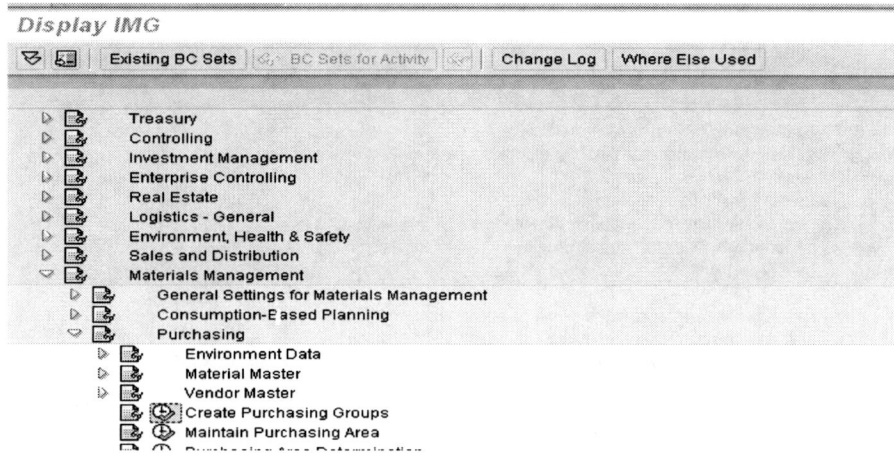

Click on New Entries

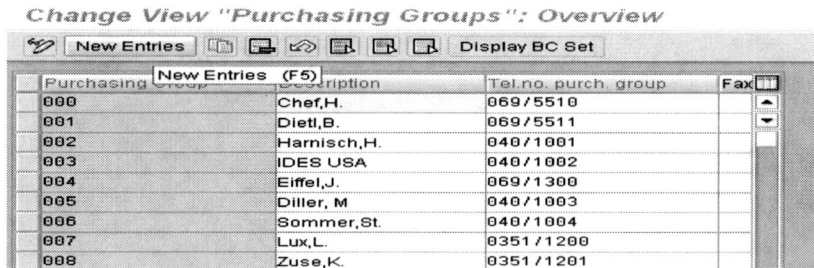

Enter the Purchasing Group, Description etc & Save

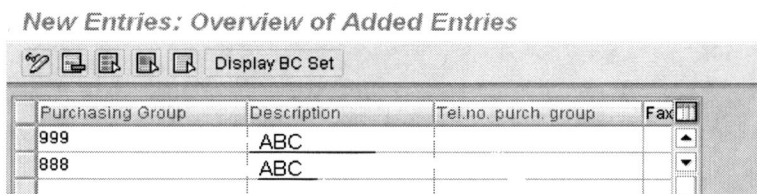

ASSIGNMENT

Assign Company-to-Company Code: -

SPRO → SAPIMG → ES → Assignment → FI A/C → Assign Company Code to Company

Select the Company Code & Enter the Company & Save it

Assign Plant to Company Code: -

SPRO → SAPIMG → ES → Assignment → Logistics General → Assign Plant to Company Code

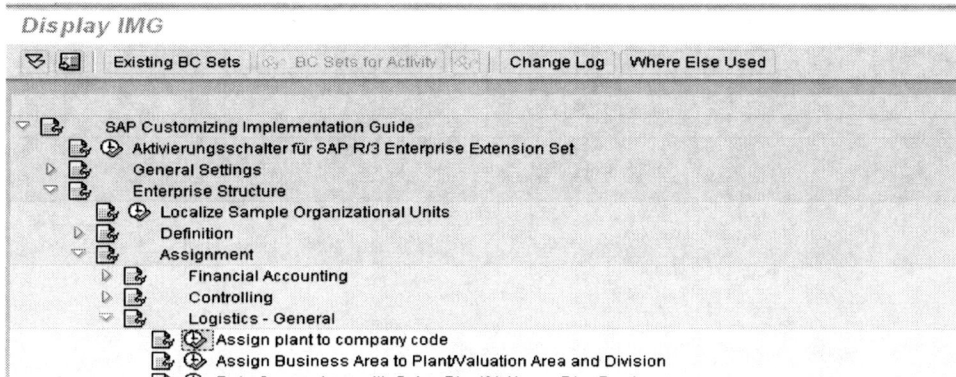

Select the Company Code & Click on Assign Button

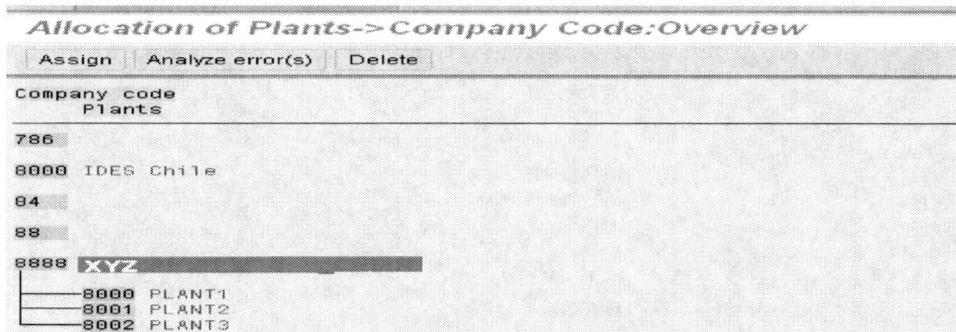

Select the Plants & Press Enter & Save

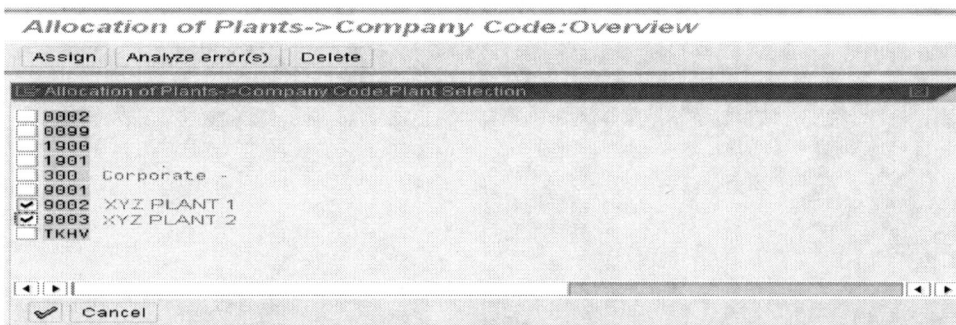

Assign Purchasing Org to Company Code: -

SPRO → SAPIMG → ES → Assignment → Material Mgmt → Assign Purchasing Org to Company Code

Display IMG

| | | Existing BC Sets | BC Sets for Activity | | Change Log | Where Else Used |

- SAP Customizing Implementation Guide
  - Aktivierungsschalter für SAP R/3 Enterprise Extension Set
  - General Settings
  - Enterprise Structure
    - Localize Sample Organizational Units
    - Definition
    - Assignment
      - Financial Accounting
      - Controlling
      - Logistics - General
      - Sales and Distribution
      - Materials Management
        - Assign purchasing organization to company code
        - Assign purchasing organization to plant
        - Assign standard purchasing organization to plant

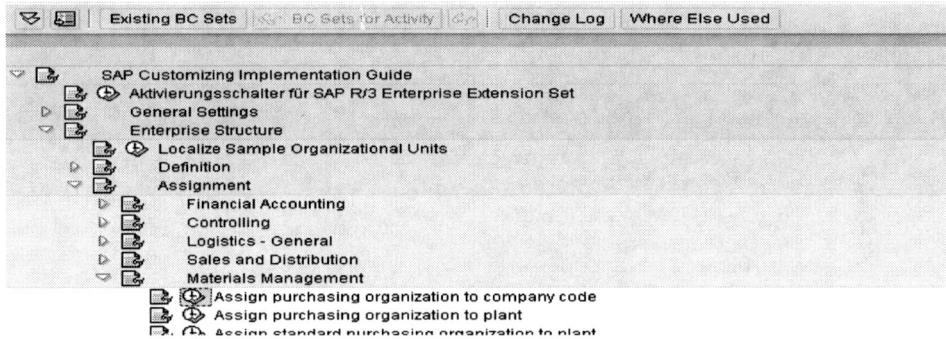

Select the Company Code & Click on Assign Button

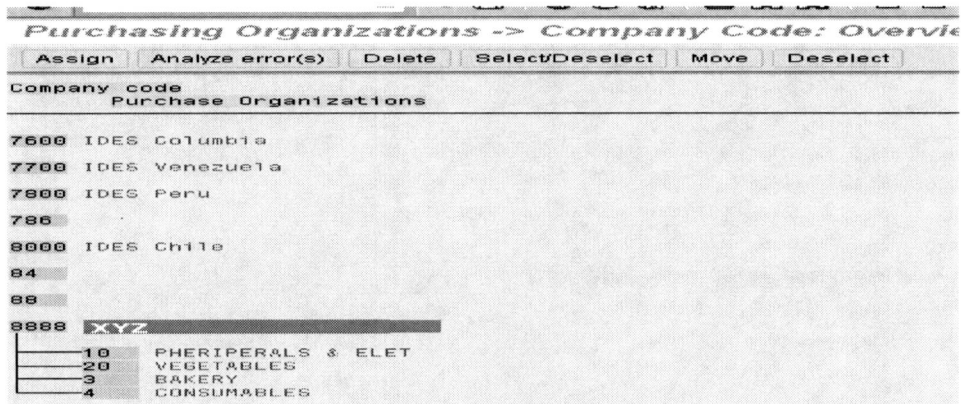

Purchasing Organizations -> Company Code: Overvie

| Assign | Analyze error(s) | Delete | Select/Deselect | Move | Deselect |

Company code
      Purchase Organizations

7600 IDES Columbia

7700 IDES Venezuela

7800 IDES Peru

786

8000 IDES Chile

84

88

8888 XYZ
```
        10    PHERIPERALS & ELET
        20    VEGETABLES
        3     BAKERY
        4     CONSUMABLES
```

Select the Purchasing Organization & Press Enter & Save it

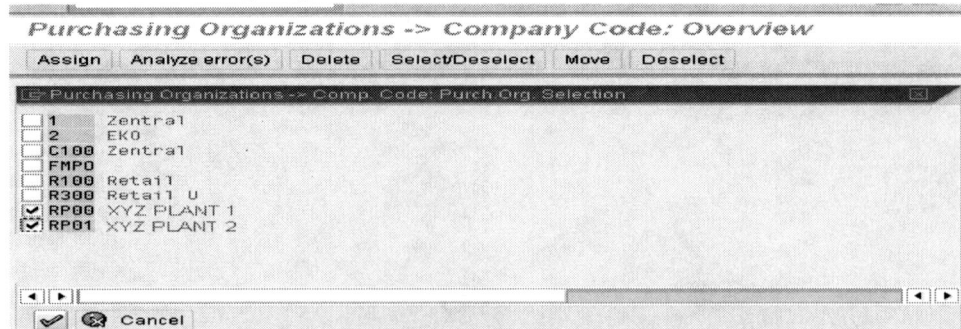

Purchasing Organizations -> Company Code: Overview

| Assign | Analyze error(s) | Delete | Select/Deselect | Move | Deselect |

Purchasing Organizations -> Comp. Code: Purch. Org. Selection

```
1       Zentral
2       EKO
C100    Zentral
FMPO
R100    Retail
R300    Retail U
✓ RP00  XYZ PLANT 1
✓ RP01  XYZ PLANT 2
```

✓ ✗ Cancel

Assign Purchasing Org to Plant: -

SPRO → SAPIMG → ES → Assignment → Material Mgmt →   Assign Pur Org to Plant

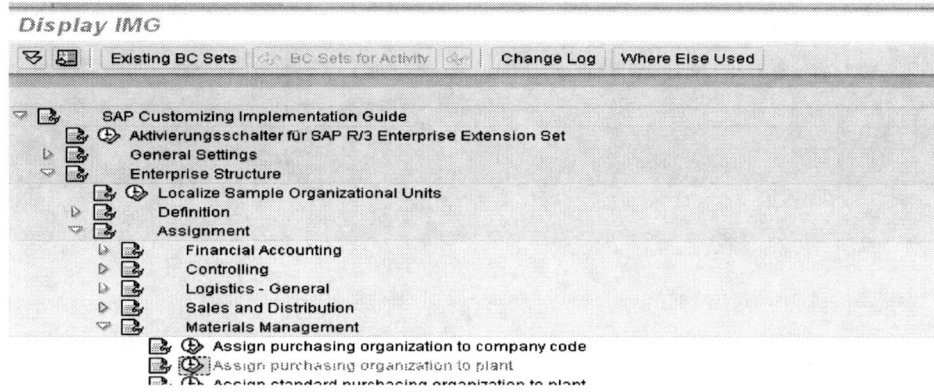

Select the Purchasing Organization & Click on Assign Button

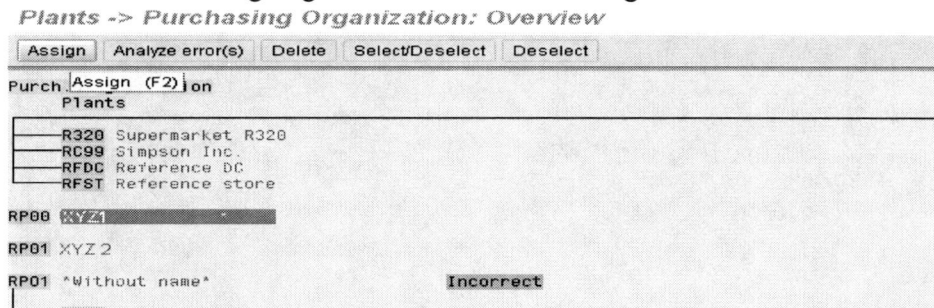

Select the Purchasing Organizations & Press Enter & Save it

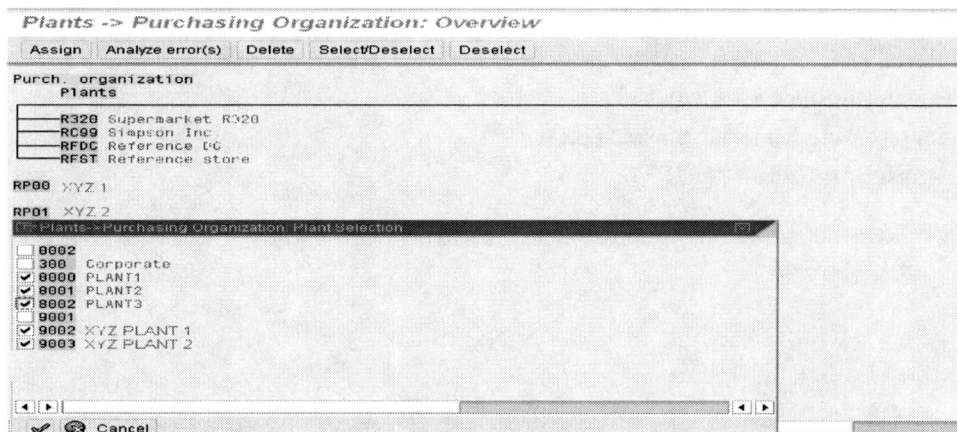

After performing all the customizing steps, view our org structure. Transaction Code: - EC01

EC01 → Structure → Navigation → Press Enter → Displays the company code → select the company code → click on details option or double click on company code, it will displays the company structure.

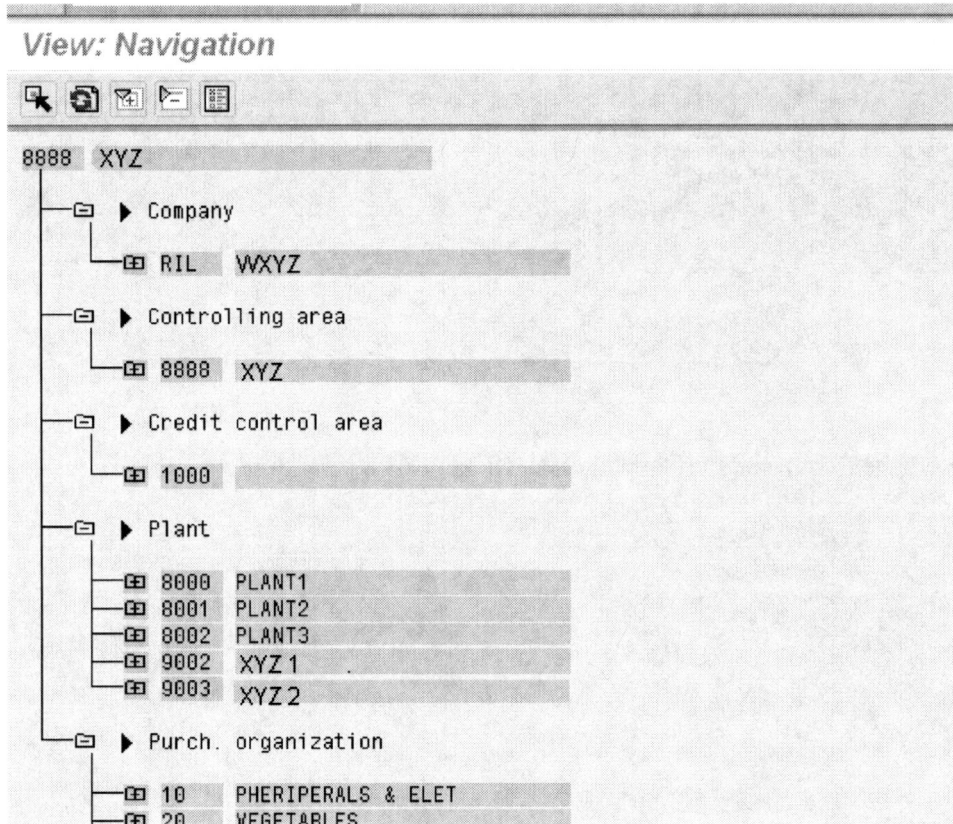

```
View: Navigation

🔍 🔄 📝 📑 📋

8888  XYZ
      ├─📁 ▶ Company
      │     └─📧 RIL    WXYZ
      ├─📁 ▶ Controlling area
      │     └─📧 8888   XYZ
      ├─📁 ▶ Credit control area
      │     └─📧 1000
      ├─📁 ▶ Plant
      │     ├─📧 8000  PLANT1
      │     ├─📧 8001  PLANT2
      │     ├─📧 8002  PLANT3
      │     ├─📧 9002  XYZ1
      │     └─📧 9003  XYZ2
      └─📁 ▶ Purch. organization
            ├─📧 10    PHERIPERALS & ELET
            └─📧 20    VEGETABLES
```

Note: -

As soon as company code is created, change the Fiscal year & month but before creating Material Master.

Transaction Code – OMSY

After Creating Material Master Use

Transaction Code - MMPV

MASTER DATA

Master data contains information, stores in a database for longer period of time and it is used for different application.

- **Different types of Master Data in SAP MM are: -**

    1. Material Master
    2. Vendor Master
    3. Info Records
    4. Source list
    5. Quota Arrangement

Material: - The goods that are subject of business activities. The material can be traded, used in manufacture, consumed, or produced

Material Master: -

It is a Master file which contains information of a particular material, depending upon the views selected from the user departments.

- **Different types of views available are**

    1. Basic data 1 & 2
    2. Purchasing
    3. General plant data storage 1 & 2
    4. Warehouse Management 1 & 2
    5. MRP (Material required planning) 1,2,3,4
    6. Accounting 1 & 2
    7. Costing 1 & 2
    8. Quality Management
    9. Plant Stock
    10. Storage Location Stock
    11. Classification
    12. Forecasting
    13. Purchase Order Text
    14. Foreign Trade: Import Data

Material Type: -

It is a key that assigns the material to a group of materials such as Raw materials, trading goods. This allows you to manage different materials in a uniform manner in accordance with your company's requirements.

The Material type defines certain attributes of the material and has important control functions.

<u>Use</u>

When creating a material master record, the material type determines

- Whether the material number is assigned internally or externally
- From which number range interval the material number comes
- Which screens are displayed
- The order in which screens are displayed
- Which department-specific data is displayed for the user to enter

- **Different Material Types available: -**

ROH	-	Raw Material
FERT	-	Finished Product
HALB	-	Semi finished Product
HAWA	-	Trading goods
DIEN	-	Services
ERSA	-	Spare Parts
PIPE	-	Pipeline material
LEIH	-	Returnable Packaging
HERS	-	Manufacturer Parts
FGTR	-	Drinks
FOOD	-	Foods
FRIP	-	Perishable Goods

Configurable materials (KMAT): Configurable materials are materials that can have different variants. For example, an automobile can have different types of paintwork, trim, and engine.

Finished products (FERT): Finished products are produced in-house. Since they cannot be ordered by Purchasing, a material master record of this material type does not contain purchasing data

Non-stock materials (NLAG): Non-stock materials are not held in stock because they are consumed immediately.

Non-valuated materials (UNBW): Non-valuated materials are managed on a quantity basis, but not by value.

Packaging materials (VERP): Packaging materials are used to transport goods and come with the goods free of charge. A material master record of this material type is managed on both a quantity basis and value basis.

Pipeline materials (PIPE): Materials such as oil, power, or water that flow into the production process directly from a pipeline, line, or other type of conduit. Since pipeline materials are always available, they are not planned.

Raw materials (ROH): Raw materials are always procured externally and then processed. A material master record of this type contains purchasing data, but not sales data since they cannot be sold.

Semi finished products (HALB): Semi finished products can be procured externally and manufactured in-house. The company then processes them.
A material master record of this material type can contain both purchasing and work scheduling data.

Services (DIEN): Services can be performed internally or procured externally (outsourced). They cannot be stored or transported.

Spare parts (ERSA): Spare parts are used to replace defective parts. They may be kept in stock. A material master record of this material type can contain purchasing data, but not sales data.

Trading goods (HAWA): Trading goods are always procured externally and then sold. A material master record of this material type can contain purchasing data and sales data.

Material Group: -T Code WG21

Key that you use to group together several **materials** or **services** with the same attributes, and to assign them to a particular material group.

SPRO → IMG → Logistic General → Material Group → Create Material Group

Price Control: - Two types of Price Controlled given by SAP

1. Moving Price – 'V'
2. Standard Price- 'S'

Standard Price:

Valuation using a standard price has the following features:

- All inventory postings are carried out at the standard price.
- Variances are posted to price difference accounts
- Variances are updated
- Price changes can be monitored

If a material is assigned a standard price (S), the value of the material is always calculated at this price. If goods movements or invoice receipts contain a price that differs from the standard price, the differences are posted to a price difference account. The variance is not taken into account in valuation.

Moving Average Price:

Valuation using a moving average price results in the following:

- Goods receipts are posted at the goods receipt value.
- The price in the material master is adjusted to the delivered price.
- Price differences occur only in exceptional circumstances.

If a material is assigned a moving average price (MAP), the price is automatically adjusted in the material master record when price variances occur. If goods movements or invoice receipts are posted using a price that differs from the moving average price, the differences are posted to the stock account; as a result, the moving average price and the value of the stock change

Valuation Class: - (For creation T Code OMSK)

It is used to determine which stock account is updated during the goods movement of a material. It is maintained in Accounting 1 view in material master record.

For material type ROH take valuation class as 3000, 3001, 3002, 3003

For material type HAWA take valuation class as 3100, 3010

For material type FERT take valuation class as 7920.

For material type HALB take valuation class as 7900. 7910

For material type DIEN take valuation class as 3200

For material type ERSA take valuation class as 3040

Number Ranges: -

Number ranges are maintained for each & every document, Posted in the SAP System. The maximum numbers of digit allowed are 18digits (99, 9999, 9999, 9999, and 9999).

Two types of number ranges: -

Internal number ranges - System will automatically define numbers to all documents

External number ranges - User has to give doc number externally while creating document.

Customize settings for creating Material Types: -

SPRO→ SAPIMG → Logistics General →Material Master → Basic Settings → Material Type

- Define Attributes of Material Type
- Define Number Ranges for Each Material Type

- **Define Attributes of Material Type**

Select the material type e.g. ROH → click on copy button

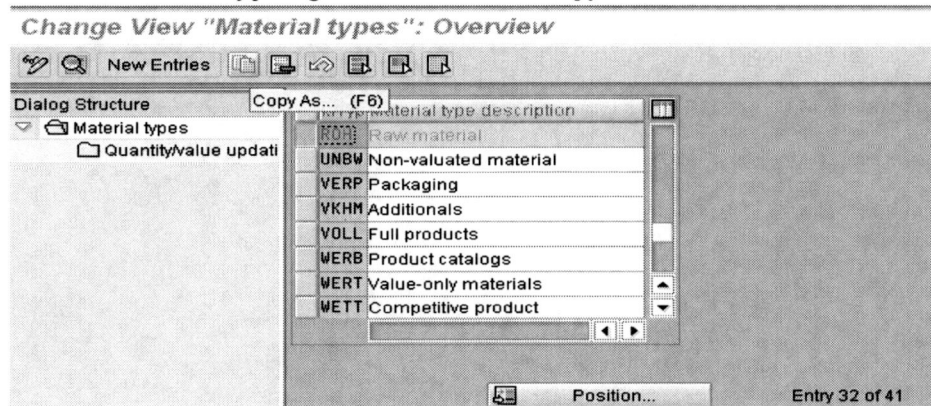

Change the Material Type from ROH to say RIL (Information technology)
Keep External Number Assignment without check

External Purchase Order – 2

Internal/external purchase order:		Ex	Ex	Short text
Ext. purchase orders	2		0	No external purchase orders allowed
Int. purchase orders	0		1	External purchase orders allowed, but warning issued
			2	External purchase orders allowed

Internal Purchase Order – 0

Internal/external purchase orde			Short Text
Ext. purchase orders	2	0	No internal purchase orders allowed
Int. purchase orders	0	1	Internal purchase orders allowed, but warning issued
		2	Internal purchase orders allowed

Change View "Material types": Details

| 🖉 New Entries | 🗋 🖫 🖄 🖫 🖫 🖫 |

Material Type   RIL   INFORMATION TECHNOLOGY

Dialog Structure
▽ 🗁 Material types
　　📁 Quantity/value updati

General data
Field reference	ROH	X-plant matl status	
SRef. material type	ROH	Item category group	
Authorization group		☑ With Qty Structure	
☐ External no. assignment w/o check		☐ Initial Status	

Special material types
☐ Material is configurable
☐ Material f. process
☐ Pipeline mandatory
☐ Manufacturer part

User departments
Status description	
Work scheduling	
Accounting	
Classification	
MRP	
Purchasing	
Production resources/tools	
Costing	
Basic data	
Storage	
Forecasting	

Internal/external purchase orders
| Ext. purchase orders | 2 |
| Int. purchase orders | 0 |

Dialog Structure
▽ 🗁 Material types
　　📁 Quantity/value updati

Classification
| Class type | |
| Class | |

Valuation
| Price Control | Moving average price/periodic unit price |
| Acct cat. reference | 0005 | ☐ Price ctrl mandatory |

Quantity/value updating
Quantity updating
○ In all valuation areas
○ In no valuation area
◉ By valuation area

Value updating
○ In all valuation areas
○ In no valuation area
◉ By valuation area

Retail-specific fields
Material type ID	General material type
Time till deleted	
☐ Display material	☐ Print price

Press Enter → Save
{Account Category Reference: - It is group of valuation classes

Item Category Group: - Group of material that the system uses to determine item category for the processing of sales document.}

Again select the material type & click on Quantity / value updating (left side)

Change View "Material types": Overview

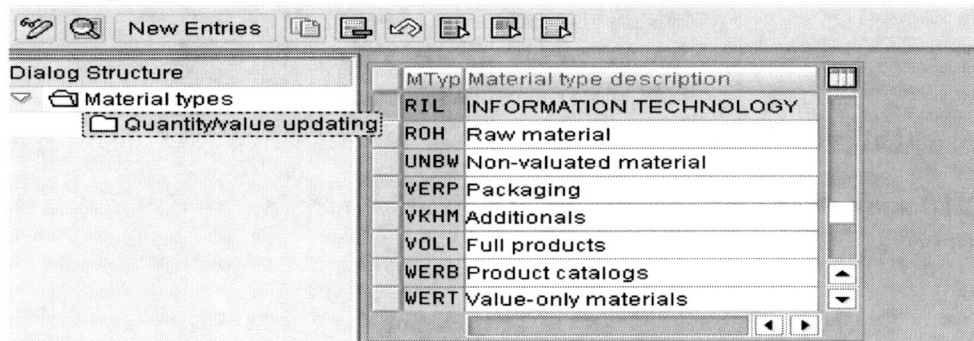

	MTyp	Material type description
	RIL	INFORMATION TECHNOLOGY
	ROH	Raw material
	UNBW	Non-valuated material
	VERP	Packaging
	VKHM	Additionals
	VOLL	Full products
	WERB	Product catalogs
	WERT	Value-only materials

Dialog Structure
▽ 🗀 Material types
   🗀 Quantity/value updating

Select the valuation area or Plant along with newly created Material type.
Activate / select Quantity updating or Value updating.

Valuation area: - Organization level at which material valuation is carried out

Change View "Quantity/value updating": Overview

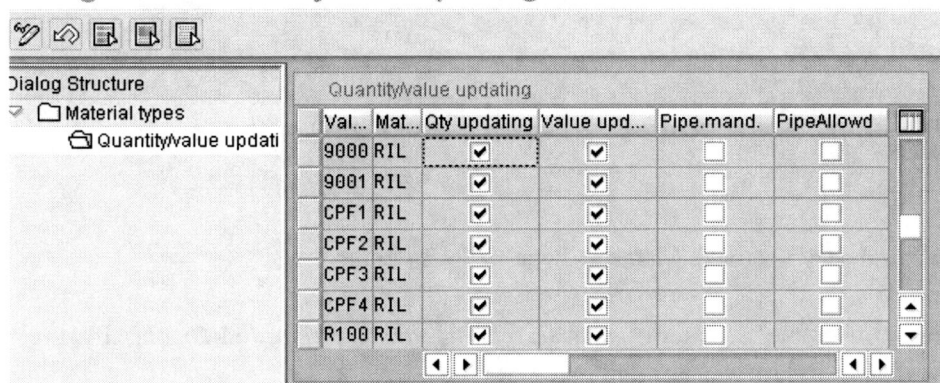

Dialog Structure
▽ 🗀 Material types
   🗀 Quantity/value updati

Quantity/value updating

Val...	Mat...	Qty updating	Value upd...	Pipe.mand.	PipeAllowd
9000	RIL	✔	✔	☐	☐
9001	RIL	✔	✔	☐	☐
CPF1	RIL	✔	✔	☐	☐
CPF2	RIL	✔	✔	☐	☐
CPF3	RIL	✔	✔	☐	☐
CPF4	RIL	✔	✔	☐	☐
R100	RIL	✔	✔	☐	☐

Then Save.

- **Define Number Ranges for each Material Type**
  Click on Groups (Maintain) – F6
  Click on Groups (Menu bar) → Insert
  Write some text
  Give number from _____ to _____.
  Select the Material Types newly created.
  Click on select element (F2)
  Select the group & click on Element / Group
  Save.

- **To Create a Material Master**

Transaction code: -   MM01 To create & to extend the material
                            MM03 To change / edit
                            MM03 To display
                            MM06 To deletes the Material master
                            MM50 To extend the Material views
                            MM60 To See Material Master List
                            MMAM To Change the Material Type

- **Path of - MM01**

SAP Easy Access → Logistics → MM → Material Master → Material → Create General

- **To Create Material Master: - Transaction Code: - MM01**

Create Material (Initial Screen)

Select view(s)	Organizational levels	Data

Material	
Industry Sector	Plant Engin./Constr.. 🗐
Material Type	INFORMATION TECH 🗐
Change Number	
Copy from...	
Material	

Select Industry Sector & Material Type → Press Enter

When you create a material master record, you are required to classify the material according to industry sector and material type.

Industry Sector
Key that specifies the branch of industry to which the material is assigned

Use: When you create a material master record, the industry sector determines
- Which screens appear and in what order
- Which industry-specific fields appear on the individual screens

Then Click on Organization levels select Views & Press Enter

Create Material (Initial Screen)

Select view(s)	Organizational levels	Data

Material
Industry Sector   Plant Engin./Constr...
Material Type   INFORMATION TE...

Change Number

Copy from...
Material

Select View(s)

View
Basic Data 1
Basic Data 2
Classification
Sales: Sales Org. Data 1
Sales: Sales Org. Data 2
Sales: General/Plant Data
Foreign Trade: Export Data
Sales Text
Purchasing
Foreign Trade: Import Data
Purchase Order Text
MRP 1
MRP 2
MRP 3
MRP 4
Forecasting
Work Scheduling

☐ View selection only on request
☐ Create views selected

| ✓ | Organizational levels | Data | Default values | ✖ |

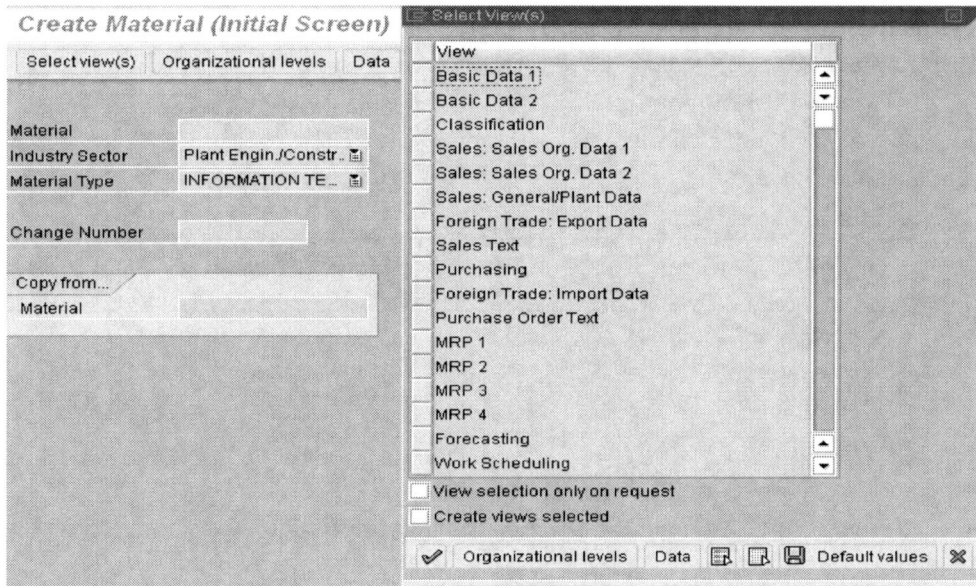

Enter Plant & Storage Location then Press Enter

Enter all the required fields in different Views (Basic data1, Sales, Accounting etc)

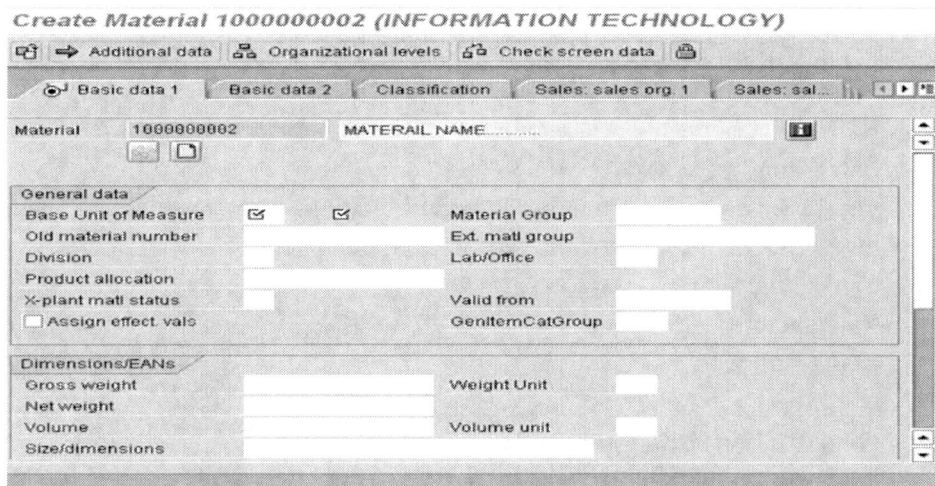

Create Material 1000000002 (INFORMATION TECHNOLOGY)

⤷ ⇒ Additional data   Organizational levels   Check screen data

| Basic data 1 | Basic data 2 | Classification | Sales: sales org. 1 | Sales: sal... |

Material   1000000002   MATERAIL NAME..........

General data

Base Unit of Measure	☑	☑	Material Group	
Old material number			Ext. matl group	
Division			Lab/Office	
Product allocation				
X-plant matl status			Valid from	
☐ Assign effect. vals			GenItemCatGroup	

Dimensions/EANs

Gross weight		Weight Unit	
Net weight			
Volume		Volume unit	
Size/dimensions			

After entering all the fields Press enter and Save

Fields in different views in Material Master

- **Basic Data 1**
  Material Description
  Basic Unit of Measure
  Material Group
  Old Material Number

X- Plant Material Status	-	Blocking option

  General item category
  Gross Weight
  Net Weight
  Volume etc

- **Basic Data 2** – contains Design Drawing information

- **Purchasing**

  Basic unit of measure
  Purchasing Group
  Material Group

Plant – Specific – Material Status	-	Blocking option

  Source list
  Batch Management – Automatic PO
  Purchasing value key
  GR Processing time (number of days required after receiving a material for inspection & then placed into the storage location)
  Critical Part
  Manufacturer Part number
  Manufacturer

- **General Plant Data Storage 1: -**
  Basic Unit of measure
  Temperature conditions
  Storage Conditions
  Container Requirements
  Hazards material number
  Batch Management
  SLED (Shelf Life Expiration Date)

- **General Plant Data Storage 2: -**
  Plant
  Gross weight
  Net Weight

Negative stock in plant
Profit Centre

- **Accounting 1: -**
Basic Unit of Measure
Valuation Class
Price control
Price unit
Valuation Category
Currency
Moving & Standard Price
Total Stock
Total Value
Division

- **Accounting 2**

Tax Price 1,2,3
Commercial Price 1,2,3
LIFO Pool

- **Work Scheduling**
Unit of issue
Production unit
Plant specific material status
Tolerance data
Material group
Batch management
Base quantity

- **Quality management**
Unit of issue
GR processing time
Plant specific material status
QM Control key
QM procurement active

Appendix 1

Material Master Related Important Terms

Material Group

Key that you use to group together several **materials** or **services** with the same attributes, and to assign them to a particular material group.

Use: You can use material groups to:
• Restrict the scope of analyses

Purchasing Group

Key for a buyer or a group of buyers, who is/are responsible for certain purchasing activities

Use
• Internally, the purchasing group is responsible for the procurement of a material or a class of materials.
• Externally, it is the medium through which contacts with the vendor are maintained.

Purchasing Value Key

Key defining the reminder days and tolerance limits valid, as well as the shipping instructions and order acknowledgment requirement of the material for Purchasing.

Procedure
If you have chosen a purchasing value key, the system enters the values defined in Customizing (for Purchasing) in the fields.

Batch

Batches (LO-BM)

A subset of the total quantity of a material in stock, managed separately from other subsets of the same material.

Example
Different production lots (such as paints, dyes, wallpapers, and pharmaceutical products), delivery lots, quality grades of a material.

Batch management requirement indicator

Specifies whether the material is managed in Batches.

Use

This indicator can be set in the material master record manually or, if batches are valuated individually, it is set automatically for the plants concerned, in which case it cannot be changed.

The indicator cannot be changed if stocks exist in either the current period or in the previous period. The reason for checking the previous period is because stocks can be posted to this period when goods movements are entered.

Profit center

Controlling (CO)

An organizational unit in accounting that reflects a management-oriented structure of the organization for the purpose of internal control.

Operating results for profit centers can be analyzed using either the cost of sales approach or the period accounting approach.

By analyzing the fixed capital as well, you can expand your profit centers for use as investment centers.

Profit Center

Key that uniquely identifies the profit center in the current controlling area.

Valuation Category

Determines whether stocks of the material are valuated together or separately.
Dependencies
In the case of **split valuation**, this indicator also determines which **valuation types** are allowed, that is, the criteria by which stocks can be valuated.

Valuation type
Invoice Verification (MM-IV)

A subdivision of a valuation category in split valuation.

Example

An enterprise manages its stocks of a material using the valuation category "Quality", comprising the following valuation types:
• 　　　High quality, Average quality, Inferior quality

Split valuation

Invoice Verification (MM-IV)

An option that lets you manage stocks of a single material in a plant in different stock accounts in terms of value. You can valuate different stocks of the same material separately.

Example

Some stocks of a material can be procured externally. Others are produced internally. Using split valuation, you can assign your "bought-out" stocks and your "made-in" stocks to different accounts and valuate the "bought-out" stocks at different prices to the "made-in" stocks. Such stocks can be subject to different price controls.

Valuation class

Invoice Verification (MM-IV)
Assignment of a material to a group of G/L accounts
With other factors, the valuation class determines the G/L accounts that are updated as a result of a valuation-relevant transaction or event such as a goods movement.
The valuation class makes it possible to:
- Post the stock values of materials of the same material type to different G/L accounts
- Post the stock values of materials of different material types to the same G/L account

Valuation Class

Default value for the **valuation class** for **valuated stocks** of this material.

Use
The valuation class has the following functions:
- Allows the stock values of materials of the same **material type** to be posted to different **G/L accounts**.
- Allows the stock values of materials of different material types to be posted to the same G/L account.
- Determines together with other factors the G/L accounts updated for a valuation-relevant transaction (such as a **goods movement**).

Pool number for LIFO valuation

Alphanumeric key uniquely identifying a pool

Use: Materials to be valuated together are grouped under a pool number.

Procedure
If a material is to be valuated in a pool, a pool must be entered in the material master record. There are two possible options:

- Pool formation via the valuation menu
In customizing for valuation, pool allocation can be set depending on material type and quantity unit. When forming a pool, the pool number is entered in the relevant material master records according to the customizing setting.

- Entering a pool number when creating or changing the material master record
A check is not made whether the pool number entered corresponds to the allocation set in customizing.

Dependencies
The pool number is only important if the field *LIFO relevant* is selected.

Valuated stock with unrestricted use

A quantity that is physically located in the warehouse, is valuated, and is not subject to any usage restrictions.

Total Stock of All Restricted Batches

Dependencies
This stock is displayed only if the material is to be handled in batches and if you have flagged the stock as restricted in the batch master record using the status key.
This stock is regarded as available in materials planning.

Hazardous material number

Number that identifies the material as a hazardous material or as dangerous goods and assigns hazardous material data or dangerous goods data to it
Use: The hazardous material number indicates that the material is dangerous, making special precautions necessary for its storage and shipment.

NOTES

VENDOR MASTER

It is a master file, which contains the information of a particular vendor. The following information is maintained in the vendor master record: -
1. Address
2. Banking Account information
3. Alternative Payee Payment
4. Terms of Payment
5. Partner function

- **Partner Function**: -
  Ordering Vendor
  Supplying vendor
  Invoice vendor

- **Types of Vendors**: -
  1. Regular Vendors
  2. Fixed vendors
  3. One-time vendors

Regular vendor: - It is a supplier of material & Services, Regularly to our Plant or Company.

Fixed vendor: -In this case we will fix the vendor for a Procurement of a material for a Particular time.

One Time Vendor: -   It is a vendor where we do business for one time.

There are three different ways to create a Vendor Master Record
- ➤ Vendor with company code: -   T. Codes   FK01, FK02, FK03
- ➤ Vendor with Purchasing organization   T. Codes   MK01, MK02, MK03
- ➤ Vendor Centrally   T. Codes   XK01, XK02, XK03

To display the list of Vendors T. Code is MKVZ

CUSTOMIZE SETTINGS FOR CREATING VENDOR

Before creating Vendor master, we have to create Account Group.
Path: -

SPRO → ***SAPIMG*** → ***Logistics General*** → ***Business Partner*** → ***Vendor*** →
Control
- Define A/C Group & Field Selection (Vendor) **T. Code**: - OMSG
- Define Number Ranges for Vendor Master Record **T. Code**: - OMSJ

Account Group: -

The account group is a classifying feature within **vendor master records.** The account
group determines:
- The number interval for the account number of the vendor,
- Whether the number is assigned by the user or by the system,
- Which specifications are necessary and/or possible in the **master record**
- **Define A/C Group & Field Selection (Vendor)**

Select the Account Group e.g. 0002

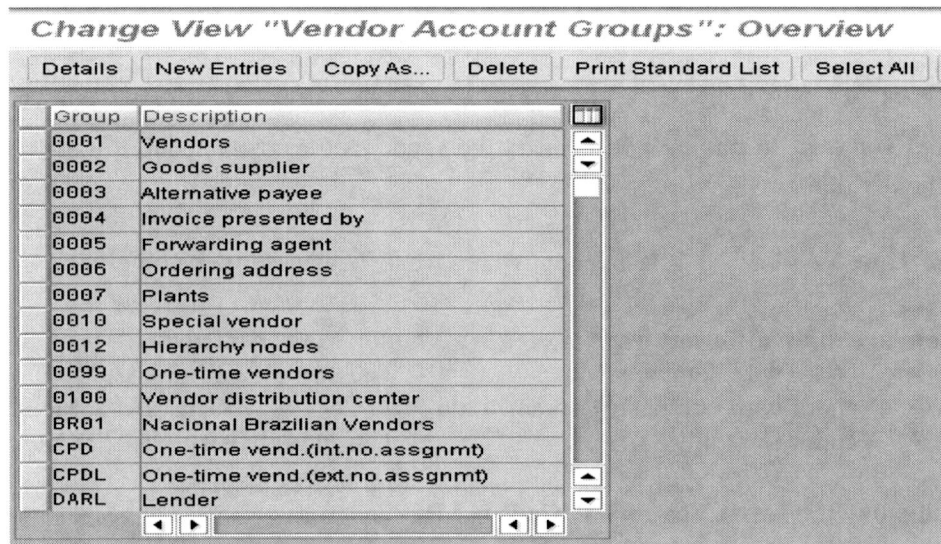

Change View "Vendor Account Groups": Overview

	Details	New Entries	Copy As...	Delete	Print Standard List	Select All

Group	Description
0001	Vendors
0002	Goods supplier
0003	Alternative payee
0004	Invoice presented by
0005	Forwarding agent
0006	Ordering address
0007	Plants
0010	Special vendor
0012	Hierarchy nodes
0099	One-time vendors
0100	Vendor distribution center
BR01	Nacional Brazilian Vendors
CPD	One-time vend.(int.no.assgnmt)
CPDL	One-time vend.(ext.no.assgnmt)
DARL	Lender

Click on Copy As Button

Change the A/C Group & Name

Change View "Vendor Account Groups": Details

| Expand Field Status | New Entries | Copy As... | Delete | Previous Entry | Next Entry |

Account Group   9999

General Data
Name   HP - WXYZ
Number Range   10
One-Time Account ☐

Field Status
General Data
Company Code Data
Purchasing Data
Purchasing Sub-Range
Purchasing Plant

Data Retent. Levels: Purchasing
☐ Vendor sub-range relevant
☐ Plant level relevant

Default Values
☐ Do not transfer any data

PartnerDetermProced.
Partner schema, purch. org.
Partner schema, sub-range
Partner schema: plant level

Press Enter & Save

Define Number Ranges for Vendor Master Record

Click on intervals

Vendor Number Ranges

Process the objects in the specified sequence

     Intervals

     Number range

Intervals → Select the Number Ranges → Enter

Maintain Number Range Intervals

Interval

Number Range Objct   Vendor

Insert Interval

New interval

No	From number	To number	Current number	Ext	
			0	☐	

Existing number ranges

No	From number	To number	Current number		
01	0000000001	0000099999		✓	
02	0000100000	0000199999	100132	☐	
03	0000200000	0000299999	200054	☐	

Go back & click on Number Ranges

Vendor Number Ranges

Process the objects in the specified sequence

    Intervals

    Number range

Select the Group & Assign the Number Ranges.

Change View "Assign Vendor Account Groups->Nu

Group	Name	Number range
0001	Vendors	01
0002	Goods supplier	X X
0003	Alternative payee	X X
0004	Invoice presented by	X X
0005	Forwarding agent	01
0006	Ordering address	X X
0007	Plants	X X
0010	Special vendor	02
0012	Hierarchy nodes	01
0099	One-time vendors	01
0100	Vendor distribution center	X X
9999	HP - WXYZ	10
BR01		X X
CPD	One-time vend.(int.no.assgnmt)	02

- **To Create a Vendor Master T. Code: - XK01**

XK01 → Enter Company Code, Pur Org, A/C group →Press Enter (fill up the fields) →Press Enter →Enter (Accounting information, G/L Account, Reconciliation A/C) → G/L Account 16000, Cash Mgmt. Group A1 → Enter (Payment Transaction A/C) → Pres Enter→ Press Enter→ Purchasing Data View (Order currency) → Enter (Terms of Payment)→ Press Enter & Save

Create Vendor: Initial Screen

Vendor	
Company Code	9999
Purch. organization	RP00
Account group	9999

Reference
Vendor	
Company code	
Purch. organization	

Vendor: Address

CIN Details

Vendor 300000

Preview   Internat. versions

Name
Title	Company
Name	HP - WXYZ
	HP

Search terms
Search term 1/2	HP - WXYZ

Street address
Street/House number	WXYZ
Postal code/City	
Country	IN India Region

PO box address
PO Box	
Postal code	

Create Vendor: Control

[icons] Tax categories | CIN Details

Vendor   INTERNAL   WXYZ

Account control

Customer   [field]   [icon]   Authorization

Trading Partner   Group key

Tax information

Tax Number 1	Tax number type		☐ Equalizatn tax
Tax Number 2	Tax type		☐ Sole Proprietr
Tax Number 3			☐ Sales/pur.tax
Tax Number 4			☐ Tax split
Fiscal address			
Jurisdict. Code	VAT reg.no.		Other...
Tax office			
Tax Number			

Reference data

Location no. 1	Location no. 2	Check digit
Industry		
SCAC	Car.freight grp	ServAgntProcGrp
Transport.zone		
Actual QM sys.	QM system to	

Person subject to withholding tax

Date of birth	Place of birth
Sex	Profession

Create Vendor: Payment transactions

[icons] CIN Details

Vendor   INTERNAL   WXYZ

Bank details

Ctry	Bank Key	Bank Account	Account Hold	C.	IBAN	BnkT	Reference Details	C..
	[icon]				⇨			☐
					⇨			☐
					⇨			☐
					⇨			☐
					⇨			☐

Bank data... [icon] Del. bk detail

Payment transactions

Alternative payee

DME indicator

Instruction key

PBC/POR number

Alternative payee in document

☐ Individual spec.

☐ Spec. per reference   Permitted payee

Create Vendor: Accounting information Accounting

[icons] CIN Details

Vendor   INTERNAL   WXYZ
Company Code   9999   WXYZ

Accounting information

Rec. Account	[icon]	Sort key	
Head office		Subsidy indic.	
Authorization		Cash mgmnt group	☑ ☑
		Release group	
Minority indic.		Certificatn date	

Interest calculation

Interest indic.		Last key date	
Interest freq.		Last interest run	

Withholding tax

W. Tax Code		Exemption number	
WH Tax Country		Valid until	
Recipient type		Exmpt.authority	

Reference data

Prev.acct no.	Personnel number

Create Vendor: Payment transactions Accounting

[icons] CIN Details

Vendor   INTERNAL   WXYZ
Company Code   9999   WXYZ

Payment data

Payment terms	[icon]	Tolerance group
		Chk double inv. ☐
Chk cashng time		

Automatic payment transactions

Payment methods	Payment block	Free for payment
Alternat.payee	House bank	
Individual pmnt ☐	Grouping key	
B/exch.limit	INR	
Pmt adv. by EDI ☐		

Invoice verification

Tolerance group

Create Vendor: Correspondence Accounting

🖫 🖺 🗓 CIN Details

Vendor	INTERNAL	WXYZ
Company Code	9999	WXYZ

Dunning data

Dunn.procedure		Dunning block
Dunn.recipient		Legal dunn.proc.
Last dunned		Dunning level
Dunning clerk		Grouping key
Dunning areas		

Correspondence

Local process.	
Acctg clerk	
Acct w/ vendor	
Clerk at vendor	
Act.clk tel.no.	
Clerk's fax	
Clrk's internet	
Account memo	

Create Vendor: Purchasing data

🖫 🖺 🗓 ⧉ Alternative data ⧉ Sub-ranges

Vendor	INTERNAL	WXYZ
Purchasing Org.	RP00	XYZ 1

Conditions

Order currency		
Terms of paymnt		
Incoterms		
Minimum order value		
Schema group, vendor		Standard procedure vendor
Pricing date cat.		No control
Order optim.rest.		

Sales data

Acc. with vendor	

Control data

☐ GR-based inv. verif.	ABC indicator	
☐ AutoEvalGRSetmt Del.	ModeOfTrnsprt-Border	
☐ AutoEvalGRSetmt Ret	Office of entry	
☐ Acknowledgment reqd	Sort criterion	By VSR sequence number
☐ Automatic purchase order	PROACT control prof.	
☐ Subsequent settlement	☐ Revaluation allowed	
☐ Subseq. sett. index	☐ Grant discount in kind	
☐ B.vol.comp./ag.nec.		
☐ Doc. index active	☐ Relevant for agency business	
☐ Returns vendor		

Default data material

Purchasing group	
Planned deliv. time	Day(s)
Confirmation control	
Unit of measure grp	
Rounding profile	

Service data

Price marking agreed	
Rack-jobbing service agreed	☐
Order entry by vendor	☐
Serv. level	

Create Vendor: Partner functions

Vendor	INTERNAL	WXYZ
Purchasing Org.	RP00	XYZ 1

Partner Functions

P..	Name	Number	Name	D..

Appendix 2

Vendor master

Vendor account group

The account group is a classifying feature within **vendor master records.** The account group determines:

- The number interval for the account number of the vendor,
- Whether the number is assigned by the user or by the system,
- Which specifications are necessary and/or possible in the **master record**

Reconciliation Account in General Ledger

The reconciliation account in G/L accounting is the account, which is, updated parallel to the sub ledger account for normal postings (for example, invoice or payment).
For special postings (for example, down payment or bill of exchange), this account is replaced by another account (for example, 'down payments received' instead of 'receivables').
The replacement takes place due to the special G/L indicator, which you must specify for these types of postings.

Incoterms (part 1)

Commonly used trading terms that comply with the standards established by the International Chamber of Commerce (ICC).

Use

Incoterms specify certain internationally recognized procedures that the shipper and the receiving party must follow for the shipping transaction to be successfully completed.

Example
If goods are shipped through a port of departure, the appropriate Incoterm might be: FOB ("Free On Board"). You can provide further details (for example, the name of the port) in the secondary Incoterm field: FOB Boston, for example

Cash management group

Use
In cash management, customers and vendors are allocated to **planning groups** by means of an entry made in the master record.

Procedure

You can define these planning groups in Customizing or the Implementation Guide (you will need to ensure that they are all the same length). In order to improve the liquidity forecast display for major customers and vendors, it can be advisable to enter their account number as the planning group.

For the planning groups themselves a naming convention should be set up to improve liquidity forecasting. In the following examples, the customer planning groups begin with an "R" for receipts, and the vendor planning groups begin with an "E" for expenses.

Examples

R1 Customers paying by bank collection
R2 Other domestic customers
R3 Customers abroad
R4 Affiliated company customers
R5 High risk customers
R6 Major customers
R7 Rental income
R8 Repayment of loans
...
E1 Domestic vendors
E2 Vendors abroad
E3 Affiliated company vendors
E4 Major vendors
E5 Personnel costs
E6 Taxes
E7 Investments

Definition: planning group

Financial Accounting (FI)

The customers and vendors in cash management and forecast are assigned to a planning group that reflects certain characteristics, risks or the type of business relationship in question, for example:
- Customer - Bank collection
- Customer - Crisis area
- Vendor: - Member of a consolidation group

This arrangement enables you to break down the display of the cash forecast according to the reliability of your forecasts regarding the outflow or inflow of cash.

Tolerance group; Invoice Verification

Settings for vendor-specific parameters in Invoice Verification. Only one tolerance group can be assigned to a vendor in the one company code.

Use

For each tolerance group you can define:
- By how much the actual value of an invoice can differ from the expected value and still be accepted by the system;
- Whether invoices can be automatically reduced.
  These settings are valid in Logistics Invoice Verification.

NOTES

DOCUMENT TYPES

There are following types of document types: -
- NB – Standard PO & PR
- UB – Stock Transport Order
- FO – Frame Work Order
- AN & AB – RFQ
- WK & MK - Contract

NB – Standard PO: - This document type is used for creating standard PO & PR during Procurement.

UB – Stock Transfer Order: - It is used when we transfer material from or supplying material from one plant to other plant with in the same company.

FO – Frame Work Order: - It is used for low value items or consumables.

Doc Types	Description	Field Selection
NB	PR	NBB
NB / UB (STO)	PO	NBF / UBF
AN /AB	RFQ	ANA
WK / MK	Contracts	WKK / MKK
LP / LPA / LU	Schedule Agreements	LPL
FO	Frame Work	FOF

Customize settings
SPRO → IMG → MM → Purchasing → Info records, PR, PO, RFQ, Contracts, S.A.
1. Define Document Type
2. Define Number Ranges for Document Types
3. Define Layout at document level

Define Document Type: -
Select document type NB → Click on Copy as → edit type & description –Press enter → enter →enter → Save

Define Number Ranges for Document Types: -
Click on Intervals → Intervals → Enter Number from__ To__ → Save

Define Layout at document level: -
Field Selection: - It contains group of field selection group in which each field selection group contains entry, optional, display, hide, suppress etc.
Field selection → Select NBF → Copy as → edit → Field selection key only → programming → save

Allowing & Disallowing Item Categories: -

Go → define Document type → select doc type → allowed item categories select & insert

Link PR to doc type

ITEM CATEGORY (I)

In terms of MM – PUR: -An identifier indicates the characteristics of an item.

The item category determines whether the following are mandatory or permitted for an item:

Material Number, Account assignment, Inventory Management in the SAP system, Goods Receipt & Invoice Receipt

In terms Advertising Management (IS-M-AM):

Characteristics that defines sales relevant features of document items including planning, pricing, production, billing etc

Item category plans a vital role in MM. It is a key, which determines how the procurement of the material & services is to be controlled for the particular item.

Depending upon the item categories the scenario of purchasing documents varies / changes.

Document types of item category: -
1. Standard
2. L – Sub contracting
3. K – Consignment
4. B – Limit
5. U – Stock Transfer
6. D – Services
7. T – Text
8. S – Third Party

Account Assignment Category (A): -

It determines which A/C Assignment data is necessary or required for the particular item

Different Types: -
1. 1 - Third Party
2. P - Projects
3. K – Cost Centre

4. A -   Asset
5. C -   Sales order
6. U -   Unknown etc.

Controlling Area: - (FI / CO)

The main function of Controlling Area is to control or capture the expenses those are incurred in the company. It mainly deals with the probability of items or material. Always Controlling Area is assign to Company Code only.

Customized settings
Maintain Controlling Area

SPRO → IMG → ES → DEF → Controlling → Maintain Controlling Area

Click on New Entries
Controlling Area = Company Code
Company Code = Controlling Area
Currency Type, currency
SAVE

Assign Company code to Controlling Area

SPRO → IMG → ES →DEF →Controlling →Assign Company code to Controlling Area

Select the Company Code
Click on Assignment of Company Codes (left side)
New Entries
Enter company code → Enter
Save

Maintain Components or Control Indicators to Controlling Area

SPRO → IMG → ES → DEF → Controlling → general controlling → Org → Maintain CA

- Select the Company code
- Click on Activate Components / Control Indicators (left side)
- New Entries
- Enter Fiscal Year
- Cost Centres → Component Active
- Order Mgmt → Component Active

- Profit Centers, Projects Sales Order, Cost Objects, All currencies
- Save
- Go back & again select on
- Company codes → Click on details
- Save
- Go back & again select company code → click on details → Save

To Create Cost Center (Department): -

SPRO → IMG → Controlling →Cost Center A/C → Master Data → Cost Center → Create Cost Center → Create Cost Center

- Cost Center   → (Give any name)
- Valid From
- Enter
- Name
- Person Responsible
- Cost Center Category
- Hierarchy Area
- Business Area
- Currency → Enter & Save

To Create Cost Element: - (G/L A/C): -

SPRO → IMG → Controlling →Cost Center A/C → Master Data → Cost Center →Cost Element

- Create Primary Cost Element
- Cost Element → 400000
- Enter
- Basic Data
- Cost Element Category
- Click on Default A/C Assignment
- Controlling Area
- Select zero
- Select Settings for each Fiscal Year

PURCHASING

1. Purchasing Requisition – Internal document
2. Purchasing Orders   - External document
3. RFQ   - External document
4. Contracts   - External document
5. Scheduled Agreement   - External document

Purchasing Requisition: -

It is a request or instruction from particular department (Cost Centre) to purchasing department to procure certain quantity of material and services. It is only one internal document in SAP-MM.

Purchasing Requisition document is divided into four parts: -

- Document Overview
- Header
- Item Overview
- Item Details

Document Overview: -

It displays the list of purchasing documents, which are created previously according to our requirement.

Header: -
Any text message or information is maintained

Item Overview: -

In this we enter material, plant, delivery date, quantity, storage location, purchasing group, A/C assignment category, Item category etc.

Item Details: -

It displays the detailed information about item overview (like Master data, valuation, source of supply, contact person, delivery address status etc)

To create PR →Transaction Code ME51N, ME52N, ME53N

Path: - SAP Easy Access → Logistic → MM → Purchasing → PR →Create

Create Purchase Requisition

| Document overview on | 🗋 📇 🔏 ℹ️ Help 🗐 Personal setting |

| Purch.requis. Stand. | | ☐ Source determination | 🔏 |

Header

	St...	Item	A	I	Material	Short text	Quantity	Unit	C	Delivery date	Matl group	Plant	Stor. I
		10	U		687	MOTHERBOARD	1	PC	D	06.06.2008	Motherboar...	XYZ 1	..

Item [10] 687 , MOTHERBOARD ▲ ▼

| Material data | Quantities/dates | Valuation | Source of supply | Status | Contact person | Texts | ◀ ▶ |

Quantity	1	PC	Delivery date	D 06.06.2008
Quantity ordered	0	PC	Req. date	06.06.2008
Open quantity	1	PC	Release date	06.06.2008
☐ Closed			Plnd dely time	
☐ "Fixed" ind.			GR proc. time	

| ME51N 🖅 | sree | INS |

To see the list of PR's: - T. Code: - ME5A

Fields in Item Details
Material Data

Material data

Material	1 000000000	☞ Short text	INTEL-MOTHERBO
Batch		Revision Level	
Material group	00202	Motherboards	
Vendor Mat. No.			

Quantities /Dates

Quantities/dates

Quantity	1	PC	Delivery date	D 08.07.2008
Quantity ordered	0	PC	Req. date	08.07.2008
Open quantity	1	PC	Release date	08.07.2008
☐ Closed			Plnd dely time	
☐ "Fixed" ind.			GR proc. time	

Valuation

Valuation

Valuation price	3.000,00	INR	/	1	PC	Total value	3.000,00	INR

Promotion

☑ Goods receipt
✔ Invoice receipt
☐ GR non-valuated

Source of Supply

Source of supply

Agreement		Purch. Organization	Order unit
Fixed vendor			Supplying plant
Info record			
Des.vendor			
		Vendor Material No.	

[Assign source of supply]

Status

Status

Processing stat	Not edited	Ordered	0	PC	Active
Block	Not blocked	Block Text			

Contact Person

Contact person

Created by	sap	Changed on	07.07.2008
Crea. ind.	Realtime (manual)		
Requisitioner		Tracking Number	
Purch. Group	999 ABC	Telephone	Fax Number
MRP Controller		Telephone	

Texts

Texts

Item texts	Any...
📄 Item text	
📄 Item note	
📄 Delivery text	
📄 Material PO text	

Delivery Address

Delivery address

Name	XYZ 1		
	Plant 1		
Street/House number			
Postal code/City	00000	Address	
Country	IN India	Customer	
		Vendor	

Purchase Order (PO)

PO is an external document created for the procurement of materials and services from vendor. The document of PO is also divided into 4 parts as PR: -

1.   **Document Overview**
2.   **Header** (Delivery/Invoice, Conditions, Address, Partners, Org. data, status)
3.   **Item Overview** (A/C assign cat, Item Category, Material, Plant, Del date, SL)
4.   **Item Details** (Material data, Confirmations, condition control, delivery, delivery Schedule, Quantities/weights, invoice)

A procurement type is defined for each of the document items. The following procurement types exist:
- Standard
- Subcontracting
- Consignment
- Stock transfer
- External service

- **There are different ways to create PO: -**

1.   Directly through transaction code **ME21N**
2.   With reference to PR
3.   With reference to RFQ
4.   With reference to info records.
5.   With reference to Contracts
6.   With reference to Cost Centre, G/L Account (cost element) for consumable items or not stock items with account assignment category 'K' (K= cost centre). (For non stock and consumables)

To Create a PO Transaction Code: - ME21N, ME22N, ME23N
Path: - SAP Easy Access → Logistic → MM → Purchasing → PO →Create

Create Purchase Order

| Document overview on | ☐ ☐ Hold ☐ | ☐ Print preview | Messages | ☐ Help | ☐ Personal setting |

| 🛒 Standard PO | ☐ | Vendor | 300000 HP- WXYZ | Doc. date | 06.06.2008 |

🗋 Header

☐ S.	Item	Per	O...	Matl group	Plnt	Stor.loc	Batch	TrackingNo	Requisitioner	IM material	Info re
	10	1	PC	Motherboar...	XYZ 1					1000000000	5300

🔍 ☐☐ ☐☐☐ ☐☐☐ ☐☐☐ ☐ Default values

🗋 Item [10] 1000000000 , INTEL-MOTHERBOARD ☐ ▲ ▼

| Material data | Quantities/weights | Delivery schedule | Acceptance period | Delivery | Invoice | Condi... | ◄ ► |

Material group	00202 ☐		Revision Level	
Vendor mat. no.			EAN/UPC	
Vendor sub-range			Cross-plant CM	
Batch	☐		Vendor Batch	☑ InfoUpdate

| ME21N ☐ sree INS |

After entering all the required information, Press enter and save it

- **To see the entire lists of PO, RFQ, Contacts, Schedule Agreement: - ME2M**

Fields in Header

Delivery / Invoice

Delivery/invoice

Payment terms		☐		Currency	INR
Payment in	days	%		Exchange rate	1,00000	☐ Exch.rate fixed
Payment in	days	%
Payment in	days net
Incoterms			☐ GR message

Conditions

Conditions

Net   1.000,00 INR

CnTy	Name	Amount	Crcy	per	U...	Condition value	Curr.	Condition value	C
PBXX	Gross Price					1.000,00	INR	0,00	
	Net incl. disc.					1.000,00	INR	0,00	
	Net incl. tax					1.000,00	INR	0,00	
SKT0	Cash Discount	0,000	%			0,00	INR	0,00	
	Actual Price					1.000,00	INR	0,00	

Texts

Texts

Header texts	A.
📄 Shipping instruction	
📄 Terms of payment	
📄 Warranties	
📄 Penalty for breach o	

Continuous-text 📄

Address

Address

Street/House number	WXYZ	🔍 Address details
Postal code/City		
Country	IN	India
Telephone		Extension	⇨
Fax		Extension	⇨

Partners

Partners

F...	Name	Number	Name	D	
VN	Vendor	300000	HP- WXYZ		

Additional Data

Additional data

Validity start	
Validity end	
Warranty	Collective no.

Org Data

Org.data

Purchasing Org.	RP00	XYZ 1
Purch. Group	999	ABC
Company Code	9999	WXYZ

Status

Status

📋 Active	Ordered	1	PC	1.000,00	INR
🖥 Not yet sent	Delivered	0	PC	0,00	INR
🚚 Not delivered	Still to deliv.	1	PC	1.000,00	INR
⌛ Not invoiced	Invoiced	0	PC	0,00	INR
	Down paymts			0,00	INR

Fields in Item Details

Material Data

Material data			
Material group	00202	Revision Level	
Vendor mat. no.		EAN/UPC	
Vendor sub-range		Cross-plant CM	
Batch		Vendor Batch	☑ InfoUpdate

Quantities / Weights

Quantities/weights

Order quantity	1 PC	Order unit <-> Order price un.	1	PC <-> 1	PC
Order qty.(SKU)	1 PC	Order unit <-> Stock unit	1	PC <-> 1	PC

Net weight	/1 PC	Net weight	0,000	/ Item
Gross weight	/1 PC	Gross weight	0,000	/ Item
Volume	/1 PC	Volume	0,000	/ Item
Points	/1 PC	Points	0,000	/ Item

Delivery Schedule

Delivery schedule

S...	C	Delivery date	Tim...	Stat. del. d...	Delivered	Purch.req.	Req...	N...	Open quantity	Sc...	R..
△	D	09.07.2008		09.07.2008					No. reminders	1 1	
										0	

Delivery

Delivery

Overdeliv. tol.	%	☐ Unlimited	Reminder 1		☑ Goods receipt
Underdel. tol.	%		Reminder 2		☐ GR non-valuated
Shipping instr.			Reminder 3		☐ Deliv.Completed
Stock type	Unrestricted use		No. reminders	0	
			Plnd dely time		
Rem. shelf life	D		GR proc. time		Latest GR date
QA control key			Incoterms		

Invoice

Invoice

☑ Inv. receipt   Tax code

☐ Final invoice

☐ GR-based IV

Conditions

Conditions

Qty	1 PC	Net	1.000,00 INR

CnTy	Name	Amount	Crcy	per	U...	Condition value	Curr.	Num...	OUn	CCon...	Un
PBXX	Gross Price	1.000,00	INR	1	PC	1.000,00	INR	1	PC	1	PC
	Net incl. disc	1.000,00	INR	1	PC	1.000,00	INR	1	PC	1	PC
	Net incl. tax	1.000,00	INR	1	PC	1.000,00	INR	1	PC	1	PC
SKTO	Cash Discount	0,000	%			0,00	INR	0		0	
	Actual Price	1.000,00	INR	1	PC	1.000,00	INR	1	PC	1	PC

Texts

Item texts	Any...	Texts
📄 Item text		
📄 Info record PO text		
📄 Material PO text		
📄 Delivery text		
📄 Info record note		

Confirmations

Confirmations

Conf. control [ ] 📄   Order acknowl. [ ]   ☐ Acknowl. reqd

Condition Control

Condition control

Conditions
- ✔ Print price
- ☐ Estimated price

Request For Quotation (RFQ)

We create RFQ to request the vendor's for the submission of Quotation for procurement of material & services. The RFQ is also called as tender & the Vendor is called as a Bidder.

Collective Number: -
It is a 10digit number used for the price comparison for the quotations. The number is maintained commonly to all the vendors or individual number can be maintained to each vendor at the time of creating Quotation.

Steps to create RFQ
1.	Create Quotations to vendors	**-ME41**
2.	Maintain Quotations for Vendors	**-ME47**
3.	Price comparisons for the Quotation	**-ME49**
4.	Create PO with reference to RFQ	**-ME21N**
5.	Goods Receipt.	
6.	Invoice Receipt.	

To Create RFQ Transaction Code: - ME41, ME42, ME43
Path: - *SAP Easy Access → Logistics → MM → Purchasing → RFQ → Create*

```
Create RFQ : Initial Screen

 ⚲  ⎙  ⊡  ☐  Reference to PReq   ☐  Ref. to outl. agreement


RFQ type              AN
Language Key          EN
RFQ date              06.06.2008
Quotation deadline    08.06.2008
RFQ

Organizational data
  Purch. Organization  RP00
  Purchasing group     999

Default data for items
  Item category
  Delivery date        T
  Plant                9000
  Storage Location
  Material Group
  Req. Tracking Number 9999
```

RFQ types AN – RFQ & AB – Request for GP bid.
After entering all the details in the fields press enter.
Required Tacking Number – (any number)

Create RFQ : Header Data

RFQ		Company Code	9999	Purchasing group	999
RFQ type	AN			Purch. Organization	RP00
Vendor					

Administrative fields

RFQ date	06.06.2008	Item interval	10	Coll. no.	9999999999
Language	EN	Sub-item inter.	1	Quot.dead.	08.06.2008
Validity start	06.06.2008	Validity end	08.06.2008	Applic. by	08.06.2008
		Warranty		Bindg.per.	

Terms of delivery and payment

Targ. val.

Reference data

Your reference   Salesperson

Collective number → (give any number of 10 digits)
After filling all the required fields press enter

Create RFQ : Item Overview

| RFQ | | RFQ type | AN | RFQ date | 06.06.2008 |
| Vendor | | | | Quot.dead. | 08.06.2008 |

RFQ items

Item	I	Material	Short text	RFQ quantity	O...	C	Deliv. date	Matl group	Plnt	SLoc
10		1000000000	INTEL-MOTHERBOARD	100	PC	D	10.06.2008	00202	9000	
20						D	10.06.2008		9000	
30						D	10.06.2008		9000	
40						D	10.06.2008		9000	

After this click on the address button and maintain the vendor address

Create RFQ : Vendor Address

RFQ		Company Code	9999	Purch. group	999
RFQ date	06.06.2008	RFQ type	AN	Purchasing Org.	RP00
Vendor	300000				

Name

Title	Company
Name	HP- WXYZ
	HP

Search terms

| Search term 1/2 | HP - WXYZ |

Street address

Street/House number	WXYZ
Postal code/City	
Country	IN India Region
Time zone	UTC+53

PO box address

Press Enter and Save it
Then go to T. Code: - ME47 for marinating the Quotations for vendors

Maintain Quotations for Vendors:- Transaction Code:- ME47

Maintain Quotation : Initial Screen

RFQ   6000000007

Enter RFQ Number → Press enter, Select item line & Click on item conditions

Maintain Quotation : Item Overview

RFQ	6000000007	RFQ type
Vendor	300000	HP- WXYZ

Item conditions (Shift+F6) ate   06.06.2008
Quot.dead.   08.06.2008

Quotation items

	Item	Material	Short text	RFQ quantity	O...	C	Deliv. date	Ne
	10	1000000000	INTEL-MOTHERBOARD	100	PC	D	10.06.2008	

Enter the Conditions, Go back & save

Change Quotation: Item - Conditions

Item	10	Material 1000000000 INTEL-MOTHERBOARD
Qty	100 PC	Net 600.000,00 INR

	CnTy	Name	Amount	Crcy	per	U...	Condition value	Curr.	Num...	OUn
	PBXX	Gross Price	1.000,00	INR	1	PC	100.000,00	INR	1	PC
	ZA01	Surcharge % on Gross	500,000	%			500.000,00	INR	0	
		Net incl. disc.	6.000,00	INR	1	PC	600.000,00	INR	1	PC
		Net incl. tax	6.000,00	INR	1	PC	600.000,00	INR	1	PC
	FRA1	Freight %	20,000	%			120.000,00	INR	0	
	SKT0	Cash Discount	0,000	%			0,00	INR	0	
		Actual Price	7.200,00	INR	1	PC	720.000,00	INR	1	PC

Price Comparison for Quotations:- Transaction Codes:- ME49

Enter Purchasing organization, Quotation number, collective number & RFQ → Execute

Price Comparison List

Purchasing organization	RP00		
Quotation	6000000007	to	
Collective RFQ	9999999999	to	
Vendor	300000	to	
Material	1000000000		

Price Comparison List in Currency INR

| ◄◄ | ◄ | ► | ►► | ✏ Quotation | 🔍 Material | 🔍 Vendor | Additional info | 🗐 |

Material Text Qty. in base unit	Quot.: Bidder: Coll. no. :	6000000007 300000 9999999999
1000000000 INTEL-MOTHERBOARD 100 PC	Val.: Price: Rank:	600.000,00 6.000,00 1 100 %
Total quot.	Val.: Rank:	600.000,00 1 100 %

After saving the above data we creates PO to the selected vendor with reference to RFQ

- **Create PO with reference to RFQ: - ME21N**
  Just Enter the RFQ number and press enter & save it

Purchase Info Records

It is a master data used to store the price of a Material w.r.t. Vendor. Whenever we create a PO with a combination of vendor & material, the system automatically store the price in the purchasing info record & also the option info update will be in activated position in the PO.

If you wish to store information of a vendor and a material as master data at Purchasing organization & plant level, then we use info records

The Info record is maintained in four different categories: -
* Standard
* Sub contracting
* Consignment
* Pipeline

To create Info record: - Transaction Code: - ME11, ME12, ME13
Path: SAP Easy access – Logistics – MM – Purchasing – Master data – Info Record

Create Info Record: Initial Screen

Vendor	300000
Material	1000000000
Purchasing Org.	RP00
Plant	9000
Info record	

Info category
◉ Standard
○ Subcontracting
○ Pipeline
○ Consignment

Enter the Vendor, material/ article, purchasing organization, plant / site & activate the Standard Position→ Press enter

Create Info Record: General Data

Purch. org. data 1	Texts

Info record	5300003996		
Vendor	300000		HP-WXYZ
Material	1000000000		INTEL-MOTHERBOARD
Material Group	00202		Motherboards

Vendor data

Reminder 1	0	days
Reminder 2	0	days
Reminder 3	0	days
Vendor Mat. No.		
Sub-range		
VSR sort no.	0	
Vend. mat.group		
Points		/ 1 PC
Salesperson		
Telephone		
ReturnAgreement		
Prior vendor		

Origin data

Certif. categ.	
Certificate	
Valid to	
Ctry of origin	IN
Region	
Number	
Manufacturer	

Supply option

Available from	
Available to	
☐ Regular vendor	

Order unit (Purchasing)

Reminder 1, 2 & 3 (Reminding the vendor for the submission of quotation after the due date)

Available from, available to; Click on Texts

Write & go to conditions, write the conditions.

Create Info Record: Text Overview

General data	Purch. org. data 1	Conditions

Info record	5300003996					
Purchasing Org.	RP00	Plant	9000	Standard	Language	EN

Info record texts

TxtType	Text	More text	Status
☐ Info record note			
☐ Purchase order text			

Create Gross Price Condition (PB00) : Condition Supplements

Vendor	Material	Purch.Org.	Plant	Info record category	Descrip..
300000	1000000000	RP00	9000	0	Standard

Validity

Valid on	09.07.2008
Valid to	31.12.9999

Condition supplements

CnTy		Amount	Unit	per	U...	Deletion...	Scales	Texts	
PB00	Gross Price		INR	1	PC		☐	☐	
							☐	☐	

Select the line item & click on the scale option.

Create Gross Price Condition (PB00) : Scales

Vendor	Material	Purch Org.	Plant	Info record	category	Descrip..
300000	1000000000	RP00	9000	0		Standard

Validity			Control data		
Validity Period	09.07.2008		ScaleBasis	C	Quantity scale
Valid to	31.12.9999		Check		None

Scales

Scale Type	Scale quantity	U...	Amount	Unit	per	UoM	PricActive
From		PC		INR	1	PC	○
							○

Scale quantity (More the quantity lesser will be the price or lesser quantity more price)
Save

OUTLINE AGREMENTS

There are two types of outline agreements: -
1.   Contracts
2.   Scheduled Agreement

Contracts: -

We create or maintain contracts for the long-term relationship with vendors for the procurement of material & services & where the value of goods & services are maintained at fixed price for a particular period of time.

Contracts are divided into two categories: -

1.   Value contract
2.   Quantity contract

Value Contract: - Document Type: - WK
In the case of value contract we negotiate the terms & conditions with vendor through a value or price.

Quantity Contract: - Document Type: - MK
In the case of quantity contract we negotiate the terms & conditions with vendor through a quantity.

The main advantage of maintaining contracts is to get more discounts from vendors.

The creation of PO with reference to contract is called **release order.**
Steps: -
1.   Create a contract
2.   Create a PO with reference to contract
3.   Goods receipt
4.   Invoice receipt

To create a Contact: - Transaction Code: - ME31K, ME32K, ME33K.

Path: - *SAP Easy access – Logistics – Material management – Purchasing – Outline Agreement – Contract - Create / change / Display*

ME31K: - Vendor, Agreement Type-'WK', Agreement date, Agreement, Purchasing Organization, Purchasing Group, Plant, Storage Location, required tracking number, acknowledge required- enter

Create Contract : Initial Screen

Vendor	300000
Agreement type	MK
Agreement date	09.06.2008
Agreement	

Organizational data

Purch. Organization	RP00
Purchasing group	999

Default data for items

Item category	
Acct assignment cat.	
Plant	9000
Storage Location	
Material Group	
Req. Tracking Number	9999
Vendor sub-range	
☐ Acknowledgment reqd	

Create Contract : Header Data

Agreement		Company Code	9999	Purchasing group	999
		Agreement type	MK	Purch. Organization	RP00
Vendor	300000	HP- WXYZ			

Administrative fields

Agreement date	09.06.2008	Item number interval	10	Sub-item inter.	1
Validity start	09.06.2008	Validity end	09.07.2008	Language	EN

Terms of delivery and payment

Payment terms	0002		Targ. val.		INR
Payment in	days	%	Exch. rate	1,00000	☐ Ex.rate fx
Payment in	days	%	Incoterms		
Payment in	days net				

Reference data

Quotation Date		Quotation	
Your reference		Salesperson	

Validity end, Payments terms, Target Value,

Create Contract : Item Overview

Agreement				Agreement type	MK	Item conditions (Shift+F6)	09.06.2008			
Vendor	300000			HP-WXYZ		Currency	INR			

Outline agreement items

Item	I	A	Material	Short text	Targ.qty.	O...	Net price	Per	O...
10			1000000000	Motherboards	100		200000		
20									
30									

Enter the material number & target quantity.
Select the item line & click on item conditions

Create Gross Price Condition (PB00) : Condition Supplements

Purchasing Document Item
00010

Validity

Valid on	09.06.2008
Valid to	31.12.9999

Condition supplements

CnTy		Amount	Unit	per	U...	Deletion...	Scales	Texts
PB00	Gross Price	200.000,00	INR	1	PC			
RA01	Discount % on ...	5.000,000-	%					
ZA01	Surcharge % o...	200,000	%					
FRA1	Freight %	200,000	%					

Enter the conditions: - PB00, RA01, ZA01, FRA1.
Press enter & Save it.

Creation of PO with reference to Contract: - ME21N

Enter outline Agreement number
Enter & save

SCHEDULED AGREEMENT: - Transaction Code: - ME31L

For delivery Scheduled Agreement T. Code: - ME38 /ME39

If a material is ordered on a regular basis and is to be delivered according to an exact time schedule, then we setup a scheduling agreement.

Vendor, Agreement Type, Date, Purchasing organization & Group, Plant & Storage location, Acknowledge required

Create Scheduling Agreement : Initia

Vendor	300000
Agreement type	LP
Agreement date	09.06.2008
Agreement	

Organizational data

Purch. Organization	RP00
Purchasing group	999

Default data for items

Item category	
Acct assignment cat.	
Plant	9000
Storage Location	
Material Group	
Req. Tracking Number	9999
Vendor sub-range	

Type	Doc. type descr.
LP	Scheduling agreement
LPA	Scheduling agreement
LU	Transp. sched. agmt.

Validity date, Payment terms

Create Scheduling Agreement : Header Data

Agreement		Company Code	9999	Purchasing group	999
		Agreement type	LP	Purch. Organization	RP00
Vendor	300000	HP- WXYZ			

Administrative fields

Agreement date	09.06.2008	Item number interval	10	Sub-item inter.	1
Validity start	09.06.2008	Validity end	09.07.2008	Language	EN

Terms of delivery and payment

Payment terms	0002			Targ. val.		INR
Payment in	days	%	Exch. rate	1,00000	☐ Ex.rate fx	
Payment in	days	%	Incoterms			

Enter Material, Target quantity, Select line item, click on item conditions, and maintain conditions.

Create Scheduling Agreement : Item Overview

	Account Assignments

Agreement			Agreement type	LP	Item conditions (Shift+F6)	09.06.2008
Vendor	300000		HP-WXYZ		Currency	INR

Outline agreement items

	Item	I	A	Material	Short text	Targ.qty.		O...	Net price	Per
	10			1000000000	Motherboards	100				
	20									
	30									

Create Gross Price Condition (PB00) : Condition Supplemei

Purchasing Document Item
00010

Validity
Valid on   09.06.2008
Valid to   31.12.9999

Condition supplements

	CnTy		Amount	Unit	per	U...	Deletion...	Scales	Texts
	PB00	Gross Price	10.000,00	INR	1	PC			
	RA01	Discount % on ...	100,000-	%					
	ZA01	Surcharge % o ...	200,000	%					
	FRA1	Freight %	100,000	%					

Go back & Save

Then raise a PO with reference to Outline agreements. For both contracts and Scheduled agreements.

SOURCE DETERMINATION

It is component is divided into two categories
1. Source List
2. Quota Arrangement

Source list:-

It is a master data & Source determination component where we list all the supply of sources (Plant / Vendor) for a particular period of time for a particular material at plant level. The main function of source list is to fix a vendor for certain period.

The source list is maintained at two levels: -

- Individually for the material / purchasing data view
- Maintained at plant level

Customize Setting

SPRO → IMG → MM → Purchasing → Source List → define Source list required at Plant level

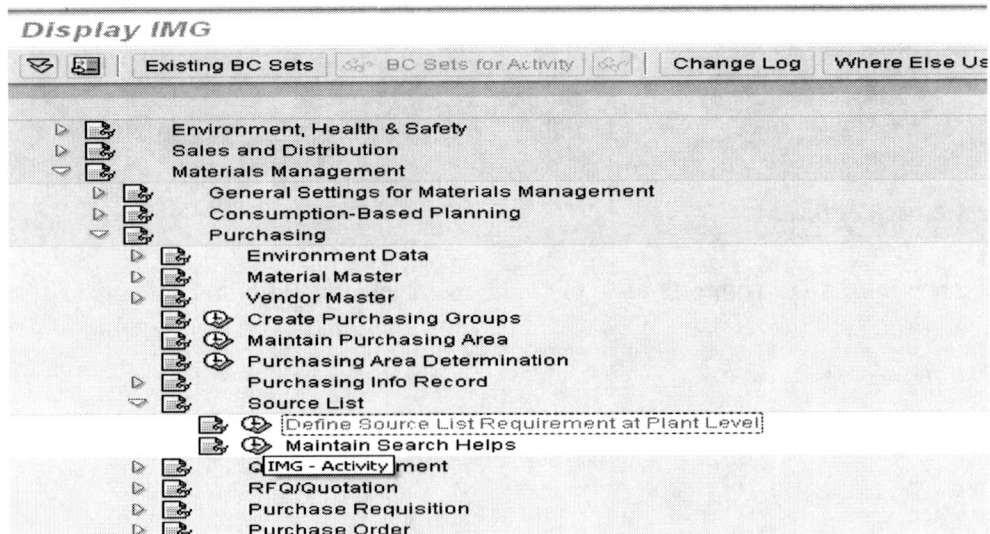

Display IMG

| | Existing BC Sets | BC Sets for Activity | Change Log | Where Else Us |

```
▷ 🗁  Environment, Health & Safety
▷ 🗁  Sales and Distribution
▽ 🗁  Materials Management
   ▷ 🗁  General Settings for Materials Management
   ▷ 🗁  Consumption-Based Planning
   ▽ 🗁  Purchasing
      ▷ 🗁  Environment Data
      ▷ 🗁  Material Master
      ▷ 🗁  Vendor Master
        🗁 ④  Create Purchasing Groups
        🗁 ④  Maintain Purchasing Area
        🗁 ④  Purchasing Area Determination
      ▷ 🗁  Purchasing Info Record
      ▽ 🗁  Source List
           🗁 ④ [Define Source List Requirement at Plant Level]
           🗁 ④  Maintain Search Helps
      ▷ 🗁  Q[IMG - Activity]ment
      ▷ 🗁  RFQ/Quotation
      ▷ 🗁  Purchase Requisition
      ▷ 🗁  Purchase Order
```

Change View "Source List/Plant": Overview

Pint	Name 1	Source list	
9000	XYZ 1	☑	▲
9001	XYZ 2	☐	▼

Here we activate the Source list option to our plant. It is possible to fix all the vendors for all the materials in a plant.

To maintain Source List: -Transaction Code: - ME01 - Create
                                                   ME04 - Change
                                                   ME03 - Display

Steps to Perform the Source list: -
- Activate the Source list record in Material Master Record.
- Maintain Source List
- Create PO
- GR
- IR

To create source list → ME01
Enter Material, Plant, Valid from, Valid to Vendor

Press enter & Save it

Maintain Source List: Initial Screen

Material	1 000000000
Plant	9000

Transaction Code MM02
→ Enter Material → Select views → Purchasing → Activate or deactivate source list & Save

Change Material 1000000000 (INFORMATION TECHNOLOGY)

Additional data   Organizational levels   Check screen data

Basic data 2 | Purchasing | Foreign trade import | Purchase order...

Plant-sp.matl status		Valid from	
Tax ind. f. material		Qual.f.FreeGoodsDis.	
Material freight grp		☐ Autom. PO	
☐ Batch management			

Purchasing values
Purchasing value key			Shipping instructs.		
Reminder 1	0	days	Underdel. tolerance	0,0	percent
Reminder 2	0	days	Overdeliv. tolerance	0,0	percent
Reminder 3	0	days	Min. del. qty in %	0,0	percent
Std del. time var.	0	days	☐ Unltd overdelivery	☐ Acknowledgment reqd	

Other data / manufacturer data
GR processing time		days	☐ Post to insp. stock	☐ Critical part
Quota arr. usage		☑ Source list	JIT sched. indicator
			Mfr part profile

Quota Arrangement: -

It is a master data & source determination component, where we list all the supply of sources (Plant / Vendor) & Assign Quota quantity to several vendors for a particular period of time for a particular material at plant level.

Quota Rating: -

It is a ratio of sum of quota allocated quantity & quota based quantity to quota. It is maintained in PR, PO, Planned Order or Production Order.

Path: -
SPRO → IMG → MM → Pur → Quota Arrangement → Define Quota Arrangement usage

Automatic PO

How Automatic PO raised

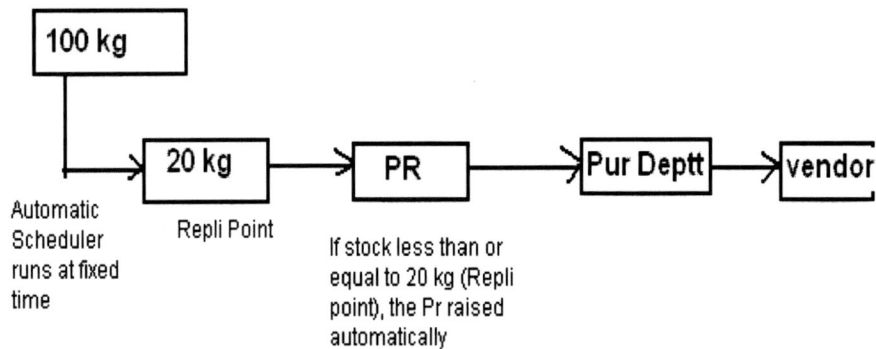

At fixed time say 12:30 AM, automatic scheduler runs and checks whether the stock is less than or equal to the replenishment point, If stock is less than or equal to Repli. Point than PR raised automatically to Purchasing Deptt

- Activate the option automatic PO in **purchasing view** in material master record.
- Activate the option automatic PO in purchasing data view in vendor master record.
- Maintain Source List & select fixed vendor
- PR crated automatically
- Automatic creation of PO from PR – ME59

Enter the Purchasing group, purchasing organization, Vendor, Plant, and Purchasing Requisition Document Number → Execute

EXTERNAL SERVICE MASTER {ESM}

We procure the different type of services from vendors they are:-

➢ Hardware & software services
➢ Construction & transportation services
➢ Machinery services
➢ Annual maintenance services
➢ Present to and breakdown service. Etc.

Service Procurement Cycle: -
➢   Requirement identification
➢   Source determination
➢   Source selection
➢   Service master
➢   Service PO
➢   Service entry sheet acceptance
➢   Invoice with respect to service entry sheet

Steps to perform services: -
      1. Create service master (AC03)
      2. Create Service PO (ME21N), with A/C Assignment category 'K' & Item Category 'D'.
      3. Create service entry sheet (ML81N)
      4. Invoice with respect to Service Entry sheet.

Customize settings
(For service category, Number Ranges & organization status for service category)

            SPRO → IMG → MM → ESM → Service Master
➢   Define organization Status for service Categories
➢   Define Service Category
➢   Define Number Ranges

Define organization Status for service Categories
•   Click on New Entries
•   Org service Category
•   BDS (Basic data service is stored in service master record under this service category)
•   CNST → Controlling Status
•   PUST → Purchasing data Status
•   SDST → Sales & Distributed Status
•   Org status description service category → Press Enter & Save

Define Service Category

- Same path as above
- Select Standard
- Click on Copy as
- A/C reference → always takes as 0006
- Enter & Save

Define Number Ranges

Click on groups → Groups → Insert → select / enter Number Ranges

Select the service category

Click on Element

Select Group & Click on Element /Group

Save

Create Service Master: - (AC03)

Click on Create New Services

Service Number(any number)

Service Category

Basic unit of measure (Hours 'H')

Enter

Basic Data → Master / Service Group → 007

Valuation class → 3200 → Enter → Save

To See the Service list → AC06

Create Service PO (ME21N)

A/C assignment category 'K', Item Category 'D'

Enter the Short text, Quantity, Delivery date, Net Price, Material group, Plant, Storage Location

Enter service number in Service Tab (Item Details), quantity price, Enter

Account Assignment → G/L Account Number e.g.400000

Cost Center e.g. 9999

Press Enter & Save

Create Service Entry Sheet: - ML81N

Select other purchase order (enter PO number) → Enter → Click on Create→ Enter Short Text → Enter → Service Number → Enter –Click on Flag button → Save

Take Service entry Sheet Number

Go to Invoice MIRO → Enter company code → Select Service Sheet Option → Enter Service Entry Sheet Number → save it.

CREATE /SETTING UP SIMPLE EXTERNAL SERVICE MANAGEMENT

Firstly -- SAP External Service Management (ESM) must not be confused with SAP Service Management (SM). ESM is the procurement of services. SM is to provide services to a client.

With External Services, you have a PO for services with Goods Receipt taking place. The Goods Receipt is called Service Entries. In contrast with goods (stock or non stock) where receiving is typically done by the inventory management group, the Service Entries are done by business themselves. The logic is that the business generated the request for the service, which is where it was done, it will be best if they do confirmation that service took place.

Let's look at the traditional SAP purchasing cycle vs. SAP purchasing cycle for External Services.

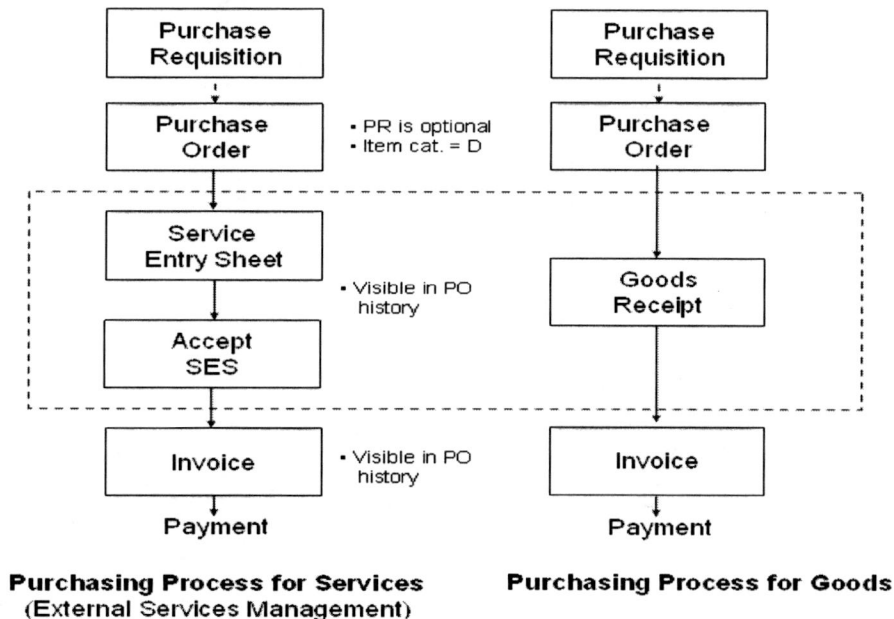

```
   ┌─────────────────┐                          ┌─────────────────┐
   │    Purchase     │                          │    Purchase     │
   │   Requisition   │                          │   Requisition   │
   └─────────────────┘                          └─────────────────┘
            ┊                                            ┊
   ┌─────────────────┐   • PR is optional       ┌─────────────────┐
   │    Purchase     │   • Item cat. = D        │    Purchase     │
   │     Order       │                          │     Order       │
   └─────────────────┘                          └─────────────────┘
            │                                            │
   ┌─────────────────┐                                   │
   │    Service      │                                   │
   │  Entry Sheet    │                          ┌─────────────────┐
   └─────────────────┘   • Visible in PO        │     Goods       │
            │              history              │    Receipt      │
   ┌─────────────────┐                          └─────────────────┘
   │    Accept       │                                   │
   │     SES         │                                   │
   └─────────────────┘                                   │
            │                                            │
   ┌─────────────────┐   • Visible in PO        ┌─────────────────┐
   │    Invoice      │      history             │    Invoice      │
   └─────────────────┘                          └─────────────────┘
            │                                            │
        Payment                                      Payment
```

Purchasing Process for Services   **Purchasing Process for Goods**
   (External Services Management)

The big difference is that the item category is D (services) is used. For the item, detail Service to be performed can be specified. The receiving is a 2 step process. Create and then Accept Service Entry Sheet

Let's step through the process and look at the documents. The steps are
Step 1 - Create Purchase Requisition
Step 2 - Convert to Purchase Order
Step 3a - Service Entry Sheet
Step 3b - Acceptance of Service Entry Sheet
Step 4 - Invoice and payment (not shown here)

Step 1 - Create Purchase Requisition

what makes the PR a ESM PR is the Item category. For goods it is blank. For ESM it is D (Service). If the item category D is selected, it is mandatory to provide the account assignment.

Step 2 - Convert to Purchase Order

The PR is converted to a PO. If me59 (automatic creation of PO) is used, the Material Group must also be entered in the selection criteria, otherwise it doesn't work.

Step 3a - Service Entry Sheet

When creating a SES, the planned services can be copied from the original Purchase Order.

Service Selection

- From current specs.
- MSS
- From purchase order   4500000606 10
  - ☐ Adopt full quantity
- From PReq
- From purch. document
- From entry sheet
- Class selection

✓ ✖

Select Services as Reference

☐ Services

Sh. text   Services Work

📂 Services

Line	...	Service No.	Short text	Quantity	Un	Gross price
10	☐	4000001	testing service master	10.0	HR	3,500.00
20	☐	4000002	still testing	10.0	HR	3,400.00
30	☐		Test service text	10.0	HR	5,500.00
40	☐			0.000		0.00

1000000330 Create Entry Sheet

🖵 Other purch. order 🔍 ✐ ▯ ▭ 🔖 🔒 🔄 🗑

Entry sheet	1000000330	◯◯◯ No acceptance	☐ Returns indicator
For purchase order	4500000606 10 🔍		
Short text	Phase One		

[Basic data | Accept. data | Value | Long txt | History]

🗎 Doc.	19.12.2005
🗎 Posting	19.12.2005
Reference	123/34
Doc. text	

Line	...	P	C	U	Service No.	Short text	Quantity	Un	Gross price
10		✓			4000002	still testing	10.0	HR	3,400.00
20		✓				Test service text	10.0	HR	5,500.00
30				✓		More work	1	EA	100.00
40									
50									
60									
70									
80									
90									
100									
110									

◄ ►

🔍 ▤ ▥ ▦ ▧ ▨ ▩ 🗎 ☐ Serv. selection   Line 10

Where:

- *P* Plan - Items copied from Purchase Order
- *C* Unplanned from Contract - Items copied from Contract (was not in PO)
- *U* Unplanned - Items was not in PO

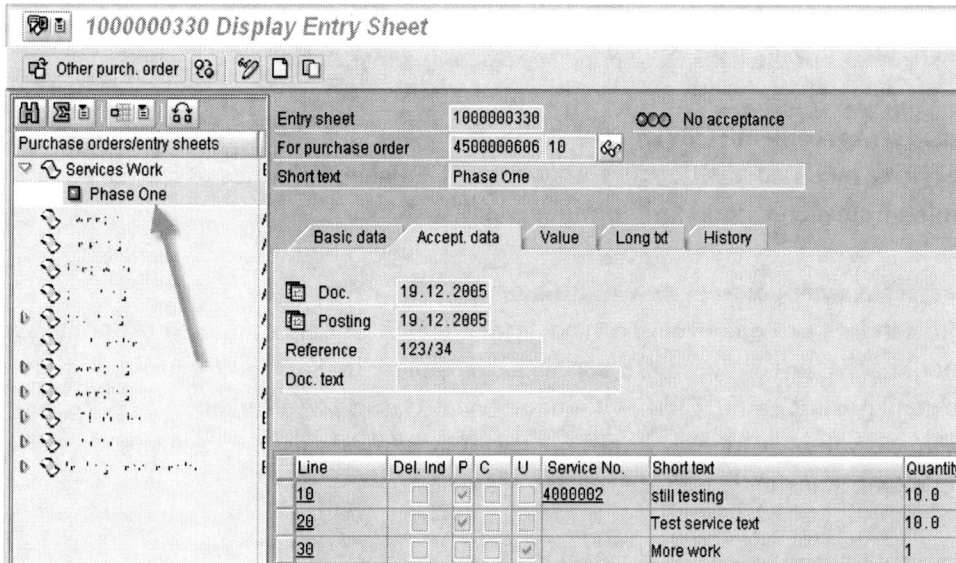

Step 3b - Acceptance of Service Entry Sheet

This is the equivalent of a Goods Receipt. The result of accepting a SES will be a material document with movement type 101 (GR against PO). Depending of process the SES can be created and Accepted by different people. Typically the acceptance is done by a more senior person.

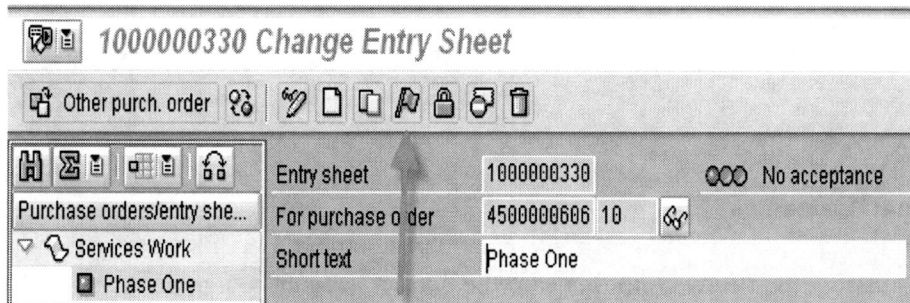

A traffic light indicate the status of the SES
- Red = Not yet accepted -- only SES
- Yellow = Accepted but still to be saved
- Green = accepted and saved

Additional notes on External Service Management

Release procedure and SES
Release procedures can be build in PR, PO and Service Entry Sheets. (Also possible on Outline Agreements and RFQ's)

Service Outlines
The services in the PR / PO can be specified in a hierarchy.

Outline Agreement (Contracts)
Services specified in PR / PO as well as Unplanned Services entered in SES can be pulled from a contract (Outline Agreement).

Service masters & Service Conditions
The services can either be free text or Services Masters (similar to material masters for goods). The prices for these services are stored in Service Conditions. Lots of SAP customers start using ESM without Service Masters. And even if Service Masters are used, one does not need to use Service Conditions. Let's look at a simple Service Master

Account Assignment U
Under special cases (if allowed), an account assignment U (Unknown) can be selected when creating the PR / PO. In this case the correct account assignment category must be provided when the service entry sheet is created.

Configuration

The focus on this post is to introduce the concept, so no configuration options are discussed. See below for config options related to this functionality.

Config Menu: *IMG > Materials Management > External Services Management*

Display IMG

	Existing BC Sets	BC Sets for Activity	Activated BC Sets for Activity	

Structure

- Purchasing
  - External Services Management
    - Service Master
      - Define Organizational Status for Service Categories
      - Define Service Category
      - Define Number Ranges
      - Field Display for Service Master
        - Define Field Selection for Service Master (Individual Maintenance)
        - Define Field Selection for Service Master (List Entry)
    - Number Ranges
      - Define Number Ranges for Service Entry Sheet
      - Define Internal Number Range for Service Specifications
      - Assign Number Ranges
    - Define Attributes of System Messages
    - Define Screen Layout
    - Source Determination and Default Values
      - for Client
      - for Purchasing Organizations
    - Maintain Matchcodes for Service Entry Sheet
    - Define Release Procedure for Service Entry Sheet
    - Formulas for Quantity Determination
      - Define Formulas
      - Specify Names of Formula Variables
    - Maintain Conditions for Services
    - Taxes at Individual Service Level
    - Messages
      - Define Texts for Service Entry Sheet
      - Form (Layout Set) for Service Entry Sheet
      - Output Control for Service Entry Sheet
    - Develop Enhancements for External Services

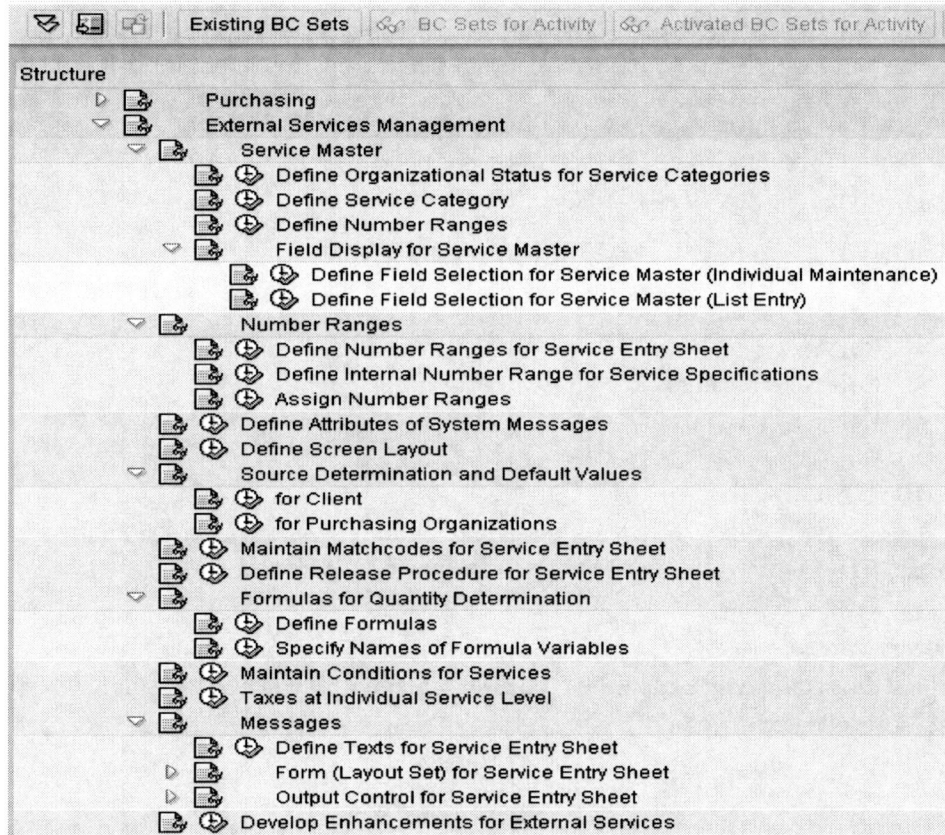

Transactions

The following transactions were used for above screens:

ME51N - Create PR
ME21N - Display PO
ML81N - Create Service Entry Sheet
ML82N - Change Service Entry Sheet (Acceptance)
AC03 - Maintain Service Master

RELEASE PROCEDURE

The main function of Release procedure is to determine the approval process or the release process for the procurement of material & services, rather than relying for manual signatures. The release procedure contains release strategy.

Release Strategy (RS)

A plan defining the release codes with which a purchase requisition item, a complete purchase requisition, or a complete external purchasing document must be released (that is, approved) and the sequence in which release is to be effected using these codes. It is a unique set of conditions, sequence and level of release.

It is a 2 digit code e.g. S1, S2, S3etc.

The Release Strategy contains the following: -
- Release Group
- Release Codes
- Release Indicators
- Release Prerequisite

Release Group: -

It is a 2-digit code, which is assigned with a class (Class contains group of characteristics). It contains one or more **release strategies**.

Release Codes: -

It is a 2digit code, which identifies the department or responsible person for the approval process & release process.

	E.g.	AA	-	Manager
		BB	-	Sr. Manager
		CC	-	Vice President
		DD	-	Managing Director

Release Indicator: -

It is a Code that represents the release status. If the proper approval process is performed that the release Strategy has to be release if it is not performed than the Release Strategy is blocked

    R – Release
    B – Blocked

Release Conditions: -

It determines the type of the release strategy
For e.g.
- If the price ranges from 1 to 1000, It is approved by AA, BB, and CC
- If the ranges from1001 to 1lac then it is approved by AA, BB, CC, and DD

Release Prerequisite

It will informs the system which RS has to be take place in the PO CEKKO is a communication structure where it displays the field names & field lengths to create characteristics i.e. we maintain characteristics in customizing by selecting the field names from this communication structure for all external documents.

CEBAN is used for the purchasing requisition.

Characteristics: -
1. Net value of PO --- GNETW (GSWRT for PR)
2. Plant --- WERKS
3. Purchasing organization -- EKORG
4. Purchasing Group --- EKGRP
5. Material group –MATKL

CUSTOMIZE SETTINGS
SPRO → IMG → MM → Purchasing → PO → Release Procedure for PO
1. Edit Characteristics T Code CT04
2. Edit Class T Code CL02
3. Define Release Procedure for PO
4. Check Release Strategy

Edit Characteristics: -

Characteristics -	e.g. NET VALUE OF VALUE
Click or Create Button	
Under Basic Data	
Description -	Value for PO
Status -	Release
Data Type -	Currency Format
No. Of Characters -	15
Currency -	EUR

Activate multiple values & Internal Values Allowed
Additional Data

Table name -	CEKKO
Field Name -	GNETW

Values
Activate Additional Values
Save the document

Create another Characteristic for Plant: -

Plant, date, Create – Description, Status
Data Type Characteristic Format
Number of Characteristics 4
Activate Multiple Values

Additional data:-
Table Name: - CEKKO
Field Name: - WERKS
Values
Activate Additional Values
For Purchasing Organization Name: - EKORG
For purchasing Group   EKGRP

Edit Class   Class   -   SAPMM
Class Type   -   032 Release Strategies
Click on Create button
Basic Data
Description   -   Class for PO
Status   -   Released
Valid From _____   Valid to _____
Click on Characteristic
Characteristic
Enter all the Characteristics Created & Save it

Define Release Procedure for PO:-
- Release Group
- Release Codes
- Release Indicators
- Release Strategies
- Workflow

Release Group: - New Entries, Release Group, Class, and Description Press Enter & Save

Release Code: - New Entries

Group	Codes	Description
99	AA	Manager
99	BB	Sr. Manager
99	CC	Vice President
99	DD	Managing Director

Press Enter & Save

Release Indicator: - (B – Blocked, R - Release)
New Entries,

Release Indicators	Description
B	Blocked
R	Released

Release Strategies: -
        New Entries
        Release Group 99
        Release Strategy S1
        Release Codes AA, BB, CC, and DD

Click on Release Prerequisites

Code wise Prerequisit	AA	BB	CC
AA		☐	☐
BB	☒		☐
CC	☒	☒	

Release Status: -

AA	BB	CC	Release Indicators	
☐	☐	☐	B	Blocked
☒	☐	☐	B	Blocked
☒	☒	☐	B	Blocked
☒	☒	☒	R	Released

        Continue
        Classification
        Enter the Value (Same Price)
        Plant (9999)
        Go Back & Save it

Release Simulation: - Simulate Release

Create a PO: -
        There are two ways to release the PO
        Individual release   ME28
        Collective release   ME29N

How to delete procedure?
        Delete   Release GP
        Create   Release RG
        Delete   R Strategies
        Delete   R Code
        Delete   R Group

CUSTOMIZATION OF RELEASE PROCEDURE FOR PURCHASE REQUISITIONS (PR).

Note: Customization of release procedure for Purchase Order & other purchasing documents are same

Release Procedures (approval) can be used for Purchase Requisitions (PR), Purchase Orders (PO), RFQ's, Outline Agreements and Service Entry Sheets. The principle is exactly the same for all. If you can master one, you will know them all.

Let's set up release procedures for PR for the following example:

Our company have got 2 plants: Plant 3100 (London) and plant 3600 (New York).
* For New York (plant 3100), if PR item value is between 0 - 1000 dollars, then PR needs to be released by one person (person B)
* For New York (plant 3100), if PR item value is bigger than 1000 dollars, then PR needs to be released by two people (first by person B, then person C)
* For London (plant 3600), if PR item value is bigger than 1000 dollars, then PR needs to be released by two people (first by person A, then person C).

Release Strategies

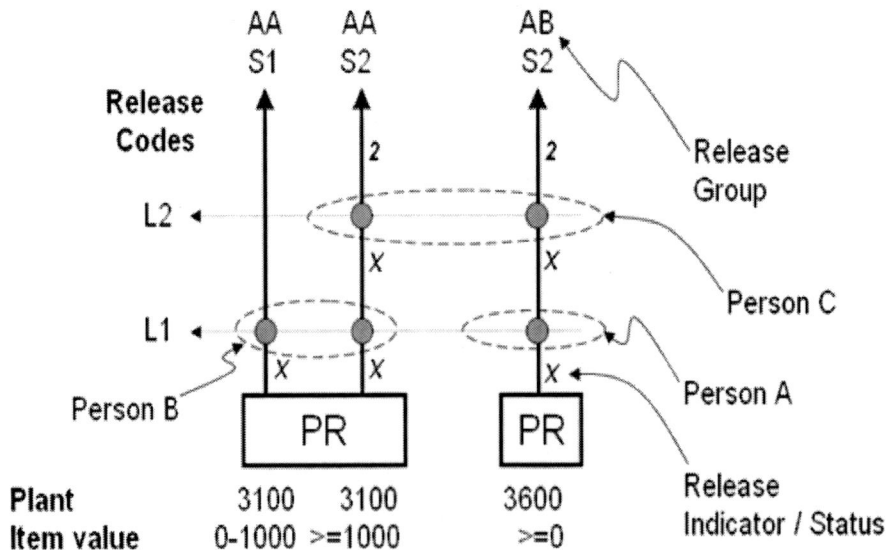

Key terminology:
* **Release Codes** - The different levels that the approval will go through.
* **Release Groups** - Grouping of strategies.
* **Release Strategy** - Unique, set of condition, sequence and levels of releases. Every line in diagram is a Strategy (so we have 3).

- **Release Indicator / Status -** The status of PR as it moves through the strategy. Example 'Block' (can't create PO yet) or 'Final Release' (can create PO from PR)

Here is a summary of the steps to follow to set up our example:

- Create Characteristics & link to comm. structure (CEBAN for PR) CT04
- Create Class & link to characteristic T Code CL02
- Create Release Groups & link to class
- Create Release Codes
- Release Indicator
- Set up strategies
  - Strategies & Codes
  - Pre requirements
  - Status
  - Assign values for strategies
- Set overall / item for doc type (PR only)
- Create and allocate authorization profiles

Create Characteristics & link to communication structure (CEBAN for PR)

Here we define which fields are used to determine the strategy that will kick in. In our case we used 'Plant' and 'Item value'. Not all fields in the PR can be used. For a full list of fields that can be used to determine the release strategy, see T.Code se12 table CEBAN.

ABAP Dictionary: Initial Screen

⦿ Database table	CEBAN	
◯ View		
◯ Data type		
◯ Type Group		
◯ Domain		
◯ Search help		
◯ Lock object		

👓 Display

Structure	CEBAN					Active
Short Text	Communication Release Strategy Determination: Requisition					

Attributes | Components | Entry help/check | Currency/quantity fields

Predefined Type   1 / 74

Com...	RT...	Comp...	Data...	Le...	D...	Short Text
BSART		BBSRT	CHAR	4	0	Purchase requisition document type
BSAKZ		BSAKZ	CHAR	1	0	Control indicator for purchasing document type
ESTKZ		ESTKZ	CHAR	1	0	Creation indicator (purchase requisition/schedule lines)
EKGRP		EKGRP	CHAR	3	0	Purchasing group
ERNAM		ERNAM	CHAR	12	0	Name of Person who Created the Object
ERDAT		ERDAT	DATS	8	0	Date on which the record was created
AFNAM		AFNAM	CHAR	12	0	Name of requisitioner/requester
TXZ01		TXZ01	CHAR	40	0	Short text
MATNR		MATNR	CHAR	18	0	Material Number
EMATN		EMATNR	CHAR	18	0	Material number
WERKS		EWERK	CHAR	4	0	Plant
LGORT		LGORT_D	CHAR	4	0	Storage location
BEDNR		BEDNR	CHAR	10	0	Requirement Tracking Number
MATKL		MATKL	CHAR	9	0	Material group
RESWK		RESWK	CHAR	4	0	Supplying (issuing) plant in case of stock transport order
MEINS		BAMEI	UNIT	3	0	Purchase requisition unit of measure
BADAT		BADAT	DATS	8	0	Requisition (request) date
LPEIN		LPEIN	CHAR	1	0	Category of delivery date
USRC1		USRC1	CHAR	20	0	User field format character for release strategy
USRC2		USRC1	CHAR	20	0	User field format character for release strategy
USRN1		USRN1	NUMC	10	0	User field numeric for release strategy
USRN2		USRN1	NUMC	10	0	User field numeric for release strategy
GSWRT		GSWRT	CURR	13	2	Total Item Value

So the two fields that will be used is:

Field CEBAN-WERKS for *Plant*
Field CEBAN-GSWRT for *Item Value*

We need to create a characteristic for every field. T.Code ct04
Any characteristic name can be used. Keep something descriptive to avoid confusion.

For Item Value -- let's create characteristic Z_GSWRT

Characteristics

Characteristic   Z_GSWRT

Change Number

Valid From   Validity

| Basic data | Descriptions | Values | Addnl data | Restrictions |

Characteristic Does Not Exist or Is Not Valid

Do You Want to Create the Characteristic?

| Yes | No |

First go to *Additional Data* tab and enter the table/field (and Enter)

Create Characteristic

Characteristic   Z_GSWRT

Change Number

Valid From   18.01.2006   Validity

| Basic data | Descriptions | Values | Addnl data | Restrictions |

Reference to Table Field

Table Name   CEBAN   Field name   GSWRT

Information

Format data taken from ABAP dictionary

Procedure for Value Assignment   User Entry Handling

Enter currency to be used in the *Basic data* tab.
Also select *multiple values* and *Intervals allowed*

The Intervals allowed will allow us to assign a range of values, example: If PR value is 0 - 1000 USD...

Create Characteristic

Characteristic	Z_GSWRT
Change Number	
Valid From	18.01.2006 Validity

Basic data | Descriptions | Values | Addnl data | Restrictions

Basic data

Description	Total Item Value
Chars Group	
Status	1 Released
AuthGrp	

Format

Data Type	CURR Currency Form..
Number of Chars	13
Decimal Places	2
Currency	USD
Template	_____ . __

Value assignment

○ Single-value
● Multiple Values
☑ Interval vals allowed
☐ Negative vals allowed
☐ Restrictable

☐ Entry Required

Save the characteristic

For Plant -- characteristic Z_WERKS

Again, the table/field name in Additional Data to enter table/field

Change Characteristic

Characteristic	Z_WERKS
Change Number	
Valid From	18.01.2006 Validity

Basic data | Descriptions | Values | Addnl data | Restrictions

Basic data

Description	Plant
Chars Group	
Status	1 Released
AuthGrp	

Format

Data Type	CHAR Character Format
Number of Chars	4
☐ Case Sensitive	
Template	

Value Assignment

○ Single Value
● Multiple Values
☐ Restrictable
☐ Entry Required

Again set multiple values and save the characteristic
The multiple values is to assign more than one plant to strategy, example: If PR for plant 3100 and plant 3600 is ...

Create Class & link to characteristic

Create a class (simply to group the characteristics). Again any name can be used. T.Code CL01 -- Create Class. The Class Type must be 032.

Configure Release Procedures

Above actions was all master data. We now need to do some configuration.
Menu: *IMG > Materials Management > Purchasing > Purchase Requisition > Release Procedure > Procedure with classification > Set up procedure*

Create Release Groups & link to class

we have two groups to create AA and AB. We need to indicate the class we are working with, in out case Z_PR.

New Entries: Overview of Added Entries

Rel.Grp	Rel.Obj.	OvRelPReq	Class	Description
AA	1	☐	Z_PR	
AB	1	☐	Z_PR	
		☐		

Create Release Codes

Create all the release code / group combinations. This is all the dots in diagram above. So we have 4.

New Entries: Overview of Added Entries

Grp	Co...	Description
AA	L1	
AA	L2	
AB	L1	
AB	L2	

Later on, authorization profiles will be linked to these code / group combinations.

Release Indicator

First we create the different statuses that the PR can be in throughout it lifecycle. Later on (below), we will be linking using these statuses. Here are the standard SAP indicators; you probably wouldn't need to add any.

Change View "Release Indicator": Overview

Release ID	Description
1	Request for quotation
2	RFQ/purchase order
3	RFQ/PO no change of date
4	RFQ/PO no changes
A	Fixed RFQ
B	Fixed RFQ/purchase order
X	Blocked

We will be using two of these -- X (Block) and 2 (Released)

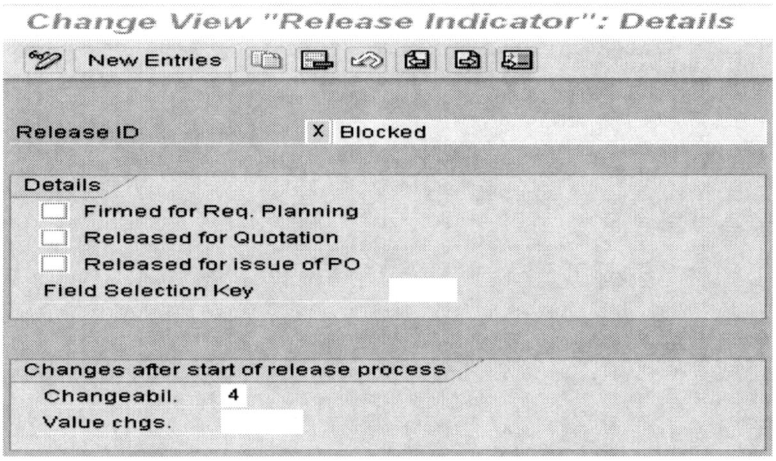

Change View "Release Indicator": Details

New Entries

Release ID   X Blocked

Details
☐ Firmed for Req. Planning
☐ Released for Quotation
☐ Released for issue of PO
Field Selection Key

Changes after start of release process
Changeabil.   4
Value chgs.

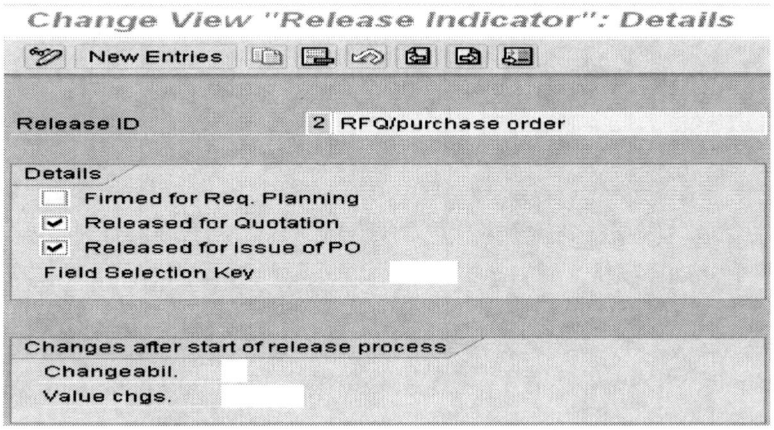

Change View "Release Indicator": Details

New Entries

Release ID   2 RFQ/purchase order

Details
☐ Firmed for Req. Planning
☑ Released for Quotation
☑ Released for issue of PO
Field Selection Key

Changes after start of release process
Changeabil.
Value chgs.

Under the Details section, you can indicate which documents can be created from this PR. For Indicator 2, one can create PO's and RFQ's. With *Field Selection* you can define which fields can be changed. This is the same indicator that gets used with document type configuration to make some fields read only, mandatory, hidden.

Set up strategies - Strategy & Codes

Every line in our diagram above is a strategy. So We have three
Lets call them:
Group AA / Strategy S1 -- Code L1 (for plant 0001)
Group AA / Strategy S2 -- Code L1 & L2 (for plant 0001)
Group AA / Strategy S2 -- Code L1 & L2 (for plant 0002)

Change View "Release Strategies

	Grp	Strat	Description	
	AA	S1		▲
	AA	S2		▼
	AB	S2		

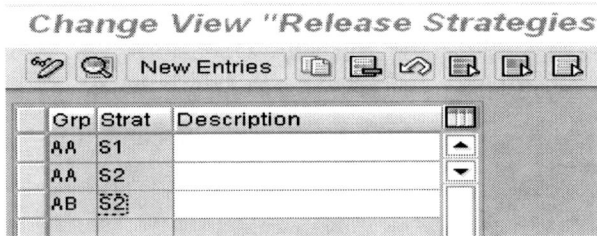

Here are the settings for AA / S2

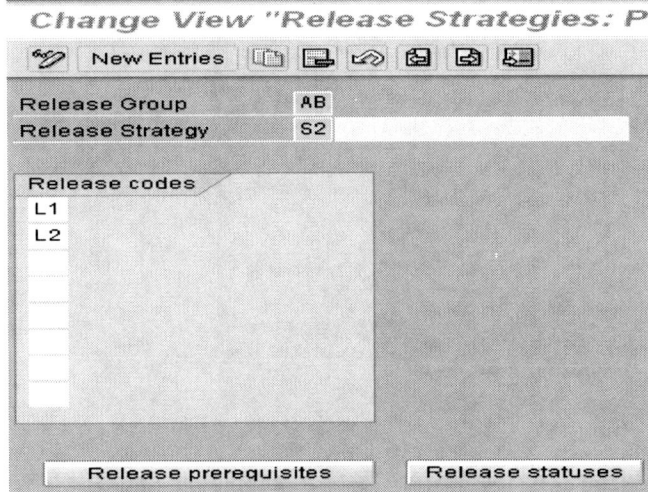

Change View "Release Strategies: P

New Entries

Release Group   AB
Release Strategy   S2

Release codes
L1
L2

Release prerequisites   Release statuses

Set up strategies – Prerequisites

Fir every strategy, we need to define a release prerequisites. This indicates if one code need to take place before the other. In this case, level 2 (L2) can only take place if level 1 (L1) has been released.

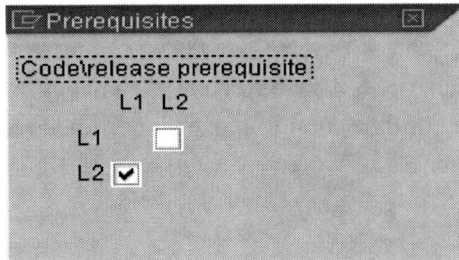

Prerequisites

Code\release prerequisite

	L1	L2
L1	☐	
L2	✔	

Set up strategies – Status

This is also done for every strategy. The screen is dependant on what groups were linked to the strategy as well as prerequisites that was set up. In this example:
- If nobody releases it then PR is block.
- If L1 release the PR, the PR is still blocked
- If L1 and L2 release the PR, the PR can be converted to RFQ/PO
Out of interest, the reason why there is not a L2 only option is because of the setting in the prerequisites.

Release Statuses

L1	L2	Release indicator
☐	☐	X Blocked
✓	☐	X Blocked
✓	✓	2 RFQ/purchase order

Continue   Cancel

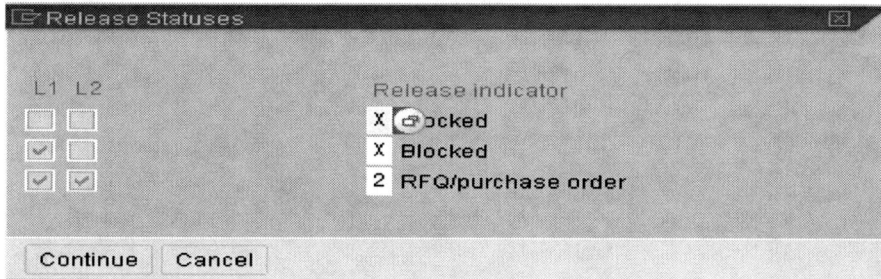

Set up strategies - Values for strategies

The values linked to strategies are master data (not configuration) and can be set in two places. Either within the configuration itself -- selecting the classification button

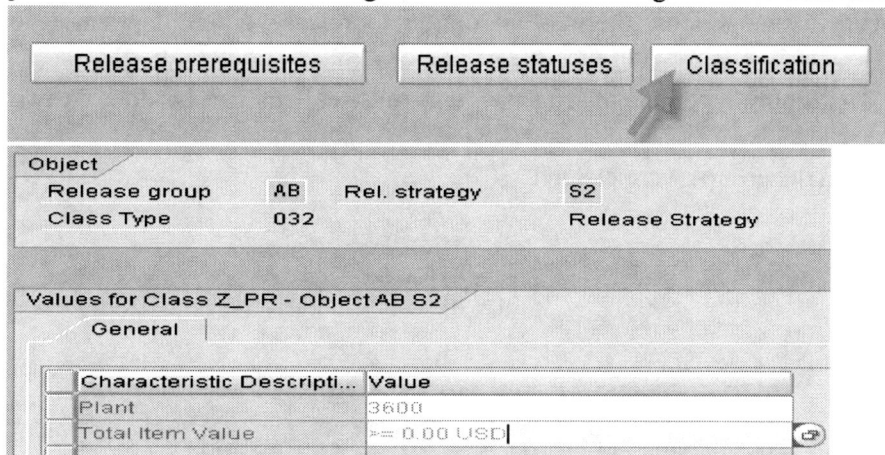

| Release prerequisites | Release statuses | Classification |

Object

| Release group | AB | Rel. strategy | S2 |
| Class Type | 032 | | Release Strategy |

Values for Class Z_PR - Object AB S2

General

Characteristic Descripti...	Value
Plant	3600
Total Item Value	>= 0.00 USD

Or, in classification, example CL24N

Assign Objects/Classes to Class

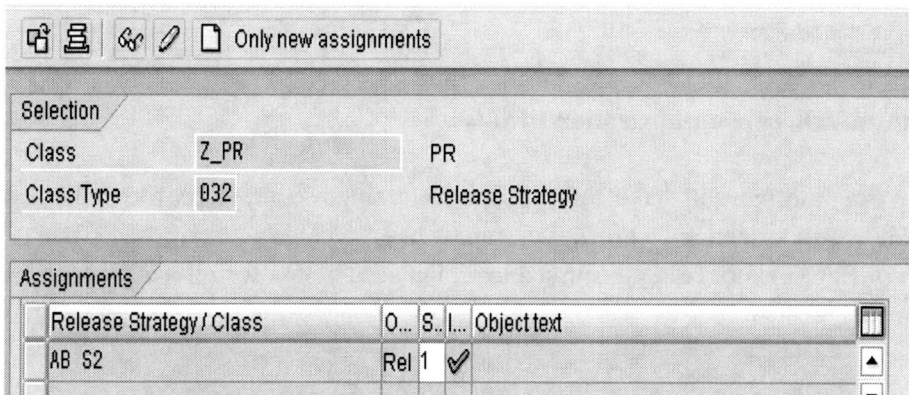

Only new assignments

Selection

| Class | Z_PR | PR |
| Class Type | 032 | Release Strategy |

Assignments

Release Strategy / Class	O...	S..	I...	Object text
AB S2	Rel	1	✓	

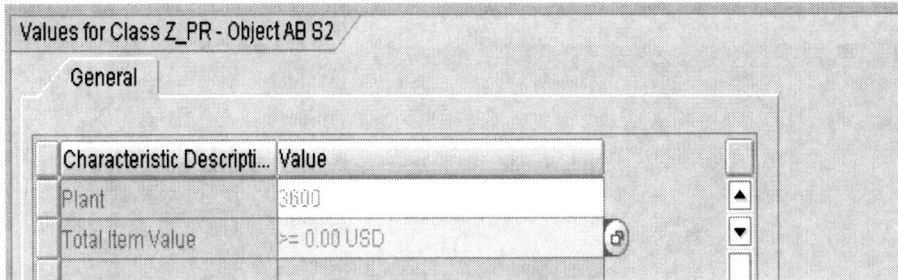

Values for Class Z_PR - Object AB S2

General

Characteristic Descripti...	Value
Plant	3600
Total Item Value	>= 0.00 USD

both methods work, the advantage of CL24N is that all the strategies can be viewed easier.

Set overall / item for doc type (PR only)

For Purchase Requisitions, there is an option to release either on item level or on document level. For PO / RFQ / Contracts, one can only release on header level. Back to the PR, it is highly recommended to use item release. This can be done in two places.

Firstly where the groups were created

Rel.Grp	Rel.Obj.	OvRelPReq	Class
AA	1	☐	Z_PR
AB	1	☐	Z_PR

on the document type configuration for PR
Config menu: *Materials Management > Purchasing > PR > Define document types*

	Type	Doc. type descript.	ItmInt.	NoRgeInt	NoRge Ext	FieldSel.	Cont...	OvRel...
	AZ	Select Document Type				NBB		☐
	F0	Framework requisn.	10	01	02	FOF		☐
	NB	Materials Planning	10	01	02	NBB		☐

Create and allocate authorization profiles

In our example we will have three people releasing, so three profiles will need to be created. Authorization profiles can be created using T.Code PFCG. Usage of PFCG is not being discussed here, but sees below for relevant screen where the profile was created.

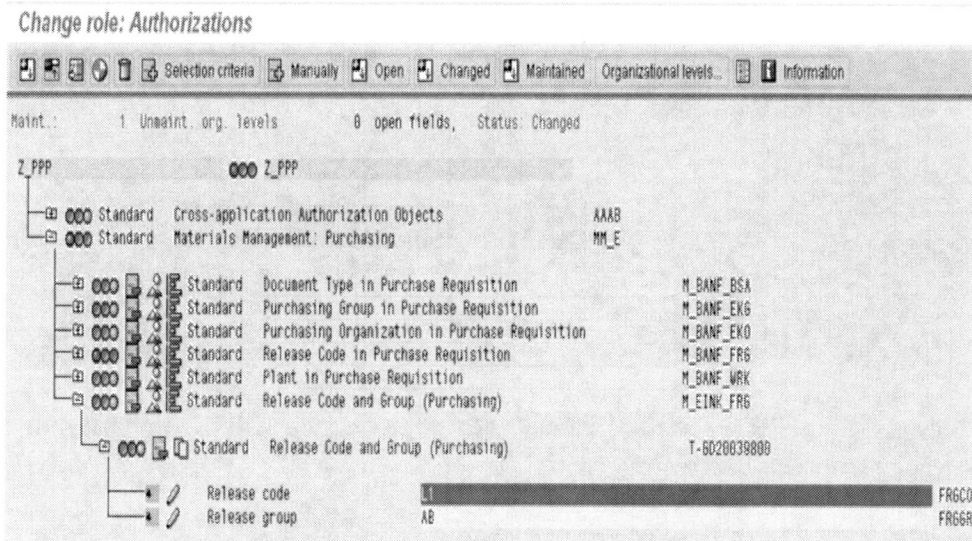

Change role: Authorizations

```
Maint.:   1 Unmaint. org. levels      0 open fields,  Status: Changed

Z_PPP                    000 Z_PPP

    └ ⊞ 000 Standard  Cross-application Authorization Objects      AAAB
    └ ⊟ 000 Standard  Materials Management: Purchasing             MM_E

        └ ⊞ 000      Standard  Document Type in Purchase Requisition       M_BANF_BSA
        └ ⊞ 000      Standard  Purchasing Group in Purchase Requisition    M_BANF_EKG
        └ ⊞ 000      Standard  Purchasing Organization in Purchase Requisition  M_BANF_EKO
        └ ⊞ 000      Standard  Release Code in Purchase Requisition         M_BANF_FRG
        └ ⊞ 000      Standard  Plant in Purchase Requisition                M_BANF_WRK
        └ ⊟ 000      Standard  Release Code and Group (Purchasing)          M_EINK_FRG

            └ ⊞ 000   Standard  Release Code and Group (Purchasing)         T-6020039800

                └ ──  ⬚  Release code       1                              FRGCO
                └ ──  ⬚  Release group      AB                             FRGGR
```

Create a Purchase Requisition

Lets create a PR, and see if the release procedure kicks in. In our case we will create it for plant 3600 and any value. So we will expect Strategy AB / S2 to kick in.

Create PR -- ME51N

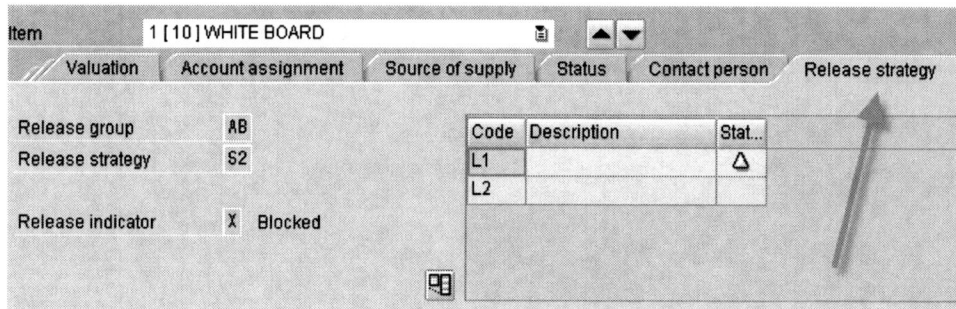

If no 'Release strategy' tab, then it didn't work. In this case all is fine. The user can see the Release Group (AB), Strategy (S2) and release indicator (X).

(SAVE)

Release a Purchase Requisition

Releasing can be done per PR or collective. Lets' use the collective release
SAP Menu: *Logistics > Material Management > Purchasing > Purchasing Requisition > Release > Collective Release -- ME55*

Collective Release of Purchase Requisitions

Release code	L1
Release group	to
✔ Release prerequisite fulfilled	
✔ Requisns. for overall release	
✔ Requisns. f. item-wise release	

Select all the items to be released and then hit save. You will see the status of the item change to the next Release Indicator.

Collective Release of Purchase Requisitions

🔍 Release strat.

Material		Short text				PGp	Mat. gp.
Requisn.	Item	Requested qty.	Un	Deliv. date	Requester	Plnt	SLoc
S C R QTy.		Ordered qty.	Un	Release date	Trackg.no.	SP1.	MC

✔		WHITE BOARD				001	001
10000581	00010		1 EA	D 20.01.2006			3600
N R X Z1	K			20.01.2006			
AB/S2		X Blocked			Release effected		

This is the absolute basics of setting up Release Procedures for Purchase Requisitions. For more posts on Release Procedures, see index of posts.

PRICING PROCEDURE

CONDITIONS OR PRICING PROCEDURE or PRICE DETERMINATION PROCESS

We deal with the Pricing Procedure for vendors.

PB00	Gross Price (info record, contract, scheduled Agreement)
PBXX	Gross Price (PO)
FRA1	Freight
RA00	Discount on net
RA01	Discount on Gross
ZA00	Surcharge on net
SKT0	Surcharge / discount
ZPB0	Rebates
MWVS	Input Tax
MWAS	Output Tax
BASB	Base Amount
RM0000	Calculation Schema or Pricing Procedure

(PB00 & PBXX)

RM0002   Calculation Schema or Pricing Procedure

(PB00)

PB00   →   AB00

Copy the Standard one and create new one (ours)

RM0000 contains all the condition types

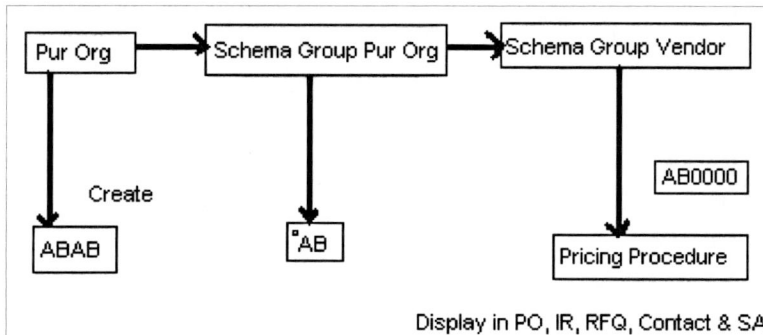

Display in PO, IR, RFQ, Contact & SA

Pricing Procedure (PP)

We define the pricing procedure to define condition supplement for the material price. The condition supplement specifies the discount, surcharge, freight etc that we want a system every time to access material price condition records.

The total value of the material is calculated or based on all addition and subtraction i.e. discounts, surcharge, tax freight etc

Condition Table

It is a table, which defines the structure of condition record key.

Condition Record

It is a data record used to store conditions or condition supplements, i.e. condition like, discount, freight, and surcharge, Tax etc.

Condition Type

It is used for different functions. In pricing the condition types leads you to differentiate different types of discounts, in output determination, batch determination, and difference between two output types, such as delivery note or order confirmation, between different strategy types

Access Sequence

It specifies the order in which system searches or accesses the condition records from condition table

Difference between PB00 & PBXX

1. Condition maintained in PB00 is time dependent whereas PBXX is time independent.
2. Condition type PB00 – used for IR, RFQ, Contract, Schedule Agreement
   Condition type PBXX – used for PO.

Calculation Schema

The main function of calculation schema is to provide framework of steps for the price determination process to specify the discounts, surcharge, freight rebate etc.

It also determines the sequence of conditions that are to be followed and in which sequence.

Schema Group Vendor

The main function of it is to identify or to pick the right process and conditions for a particular vendor.

Schema Group Purchasing Organization

Key that determines which calculation schema (pricing procedure) is to be used in purchasing documents assigned to the relevant purchasing organization.

Schema Group

It allows to group together the purchasing organizations, which uses the same calculation schema.

Steps:

1. Create Access sequence
2. Create condition types
3. Create pricing procedure or calculation schema
4. Link pricing procedure & access sequence to condition type
5. Create schema group for vendor
6. Create schema group for purchase organization
7. Assign schema group vendor-to-vendor master record in purchasing data view
8. Assign schema group purchase organization to our purchase organization
9. In inforecord purchase organization data enter condition types and pricing or calculation procedure

CUSTOMIZE SETTINGS: -

SPRO→ IMG → MM → PUR → Conditions → Define price determination Process

1. Define access sequence
2. Define Condition type
3. Define cal. Schema
4. Define schema group
   - Schema group vendor
   - Schema group purchasing group
5. Assignment of schema group to PUR org
6. Define schema determination → determine cal schema for standard PO.

BASICS OF INVENTRY MANAGEMENT

Maintaining stock by value or by quantity is called inventory. The total inventory management deals with the goods movement of the material.

Goods movement: -
It is a process in which transaction resulting change in stocks. It is further sub-divided into three categories
1. Goods Receipt (GR)
2. Goods Issue (GI)
3. Transfer Posting (TP)

Goods Receipt (GR): - It is a goods movement in which receipt of goods is posted for vendor or for production. A GR posted in the system will leads to increase in stock. No Concept of Price or value

Goods Issue (GI): - It is goods movement in which material withdrawal is posted for consumption or for customer. A GI posted in system will leads to decrease in stock.

Stock Transfer (ST): - It is method of removal of material from one location and transferring it to another location. This process is performed between two plants and two storage locations.

Transfer Posting (TP): - It is a general term of stock transfer that changes the stock type or stock categories. The difference between transfer posting and stock transfer is: -

TP is logical stock transfer and ST is a physical stock transfer.

Movement Type: - It is a three-digit code, which plays a role of important control function in inventory management. It acts as a central role in automatic account determination. It determines which stock account or consumption account is updated in financial accounting.

Reservation: - It stores requisition created from particular cost center to particular department for issuing the material reservation posted in the system. It leads to decrease in stock.

Stock Types: - The different stock types are
1. Unrestricted use stock
2. Quality inspection stock
3. Blocked stock
4. Warehouse stock

Transaction code: -

1.	To Create GR	-	MIGO
2.	To Create GI	-	MB1A
3.	For Transfer Posting	-	MB1B
4.	To display Material/GR document	–	MB03
5.	To create reservations	-	MB21, MB22, MB23
6.	To See Stock Overview	-	MMBE
7.	To enter Other GR	-	MB1C

When GR is posted in the system

Material document is created	-	MB03
Accounting Document is generated	-	MB03
MMR updated	-	MM02, MM03
PO history updated	-	ME23N

Movement Type's

Movement Types under GR - 101, 331,333,335,501,503,505,551,553,555, 561,351 (For all Movement Type's there is a reversal e.g. 101 has 102. **Note: No reversal for 121**)

Movement Type's under GI - 201, 331,333,335,551,553,555

Transfer Posting: It is performed in three ways
1. TP B/W Plant to Plant
2. TP B/W Storage Location to Storage Location
3. TP B/W Stock to Stock

Movement Types under TP B/W Plant to Plant

301	-	1 step
303 & 305	-	2 step

Movement Type under TP B/W Storage location to Storage Location

311	-	1 step
313 & 315	-	2 step

Movement Type under TP B/W stock to stock

321, 323, 325, 343,349

To Cancel the GR Movement type 102

Return delivery to vendor movement type 122 & T Code MIGO

Transfer Posting Stock to Stock

From Blocked stock to Quality Inspection
     T Code MB1B & Movement Type 349

From Blocked stock to Unrestricted Stock
     T Code MB1B & Movement Type 343

From Quality Inspection to Unrestricted Stock
     T Code MB1B & Movement Type 321

Transfer Posting from Plant to Plant

For One Step: Movement Type 301
For Two Steps: Movement Type 303 & 305
        After posting stock will display in Stock in Transit (Plant)
        To receive material by receiving Plant Movement Type 305

Transfer Posting B/W Storage Location to Storage Location

Under One Plant B/W two Storage Location's Movement Type 311
Back to Parent storage Location Movement Type 313 (It Show stock in transfer) use Movement type 315 at Parent storage location

To create Goods Issue (GI) T Code MB1A & Movement Type 201

To Create Reservations T Code MB21, MB22 & MB23

Creation of GI w.r.t Reservations

T Code MB1A & Movement Type 201
Click on Reservation, Enter Reservation Number → Click on Adopt + Details

GR w.r.t Reservations: T Code MIGO & Select as Reservation instead of GR

GR without PO Movement type 501 & T Code MB1C, Select others instead of Purchase order, Enter Material, Quantity, Plant, Storage Location → Press Enter
Partner Option will be visible (Vendor) → save it

Invoice: - Invoice is a document, which is issued to a buyer (Company) from the supplier (vendor) for the payment. The following information is maintained in invoice

Invoice date, Posting date, Invoice ref number, tax amount, amount, tax code, terms of payments, vendor address, banking accounting information etc

When invoice document is posted in the system
- Invoice document created
- Accounting document is generated (MIR4)
- PO history updated (ME23N)
- FI document created (FB03)

ERS (Evaluated Receipt Settlement)

The main function of ERS is to settle the invoice automatically by taking the information from PO & GR. The ERS option is maintained individually for each vendor in purchasing data vies of vendor master record

Subsequent Debit: - Debiting of amount to other costs to one or more business transactions, which are previously posted

Subsequent Credit: - Reduction of amount to which are previously debited to one or more business transaction posted. It is also called invoice reduction.

Credit Memo: - A posting that reduces the balance of receivables or payables.
When stocks returned back to vendor after payment has been made, then credit memo is issued to vendor stating that he is holding the payment made by us.

Transaction Codes

To Create Invoice	MIRO
To Display Invoice	MIR4
To Block Invoice	MIRO
To Release Invoice	MRBR
To Cancel Invoice	MR8M
Parking Invoice	MIR7
ERS	MRRL
GR /IR Clearing Acc	MR11

PHYSICAL INVENTORY PROCESS: -

1. Create Physical inventory document
T Code MI01 – Create single inventory document
T Code MI31 – Create multiple physical inventory documents
    I. Enter the desired fields i.e. material, material type, site, storage location, and Maximum number items / Documents – 100, etc → Press Enter
    II. Click on Process Session
    III. Select the line items and click on the process
    IV. System displays a dialog box, select Background and click on process. Inventory document is created

2. Print Inventory Document and handed over to responsible person say Manager

3. Enter Physical Inventory count
T Code MI04
    i. Enter the physical inventory document number Fiscal year, count date → Press enter
    ii. Enter the Material Quantity and click on post

4. Listing of difference
T Code MI20

Enter the physical inventory document number and execute, system displays a screen, wherein we will be able to view the differences

5. Post the differences
T Code MI07 & Mov Type 701 & 702

Enter the physical inventory document number, year, posting date, enter the difference and post

Notes

SPECIAL STOCKS & SPECIAL PROCUREMENT TYPES

Special Stocks are those stocks which are not belongs to our company code. They are not placed in our storage locations & no physical inventory is performed. They are treated as special stocks for the reason of ownership.

Different types are
1. Subcontracting
2. Consignment
3. Pipeline
4. Stock transfer
5. Third party
6. Returnable transport packaging
7. Sales order stock
8. Project stock

SUBCONTRACTING:

In subcontracting process we create subcontracting PO to supply or issue subcomponents to vendor in order to get final product. The price maintained in subcontracting PO is a service charge paid to vendor.

Steps to perform subcontracting:

1. Create subcontracting inforecord (Optional)
2. Create subcontracting PO with item category L,
   There are to ways to supply subcomponents to vendor
   - Manually maintain the subcomponents in the subcontracting PO though explode BOM
   - Through BOM (Bill of material) T Code CS01, CS02 & CS03
3. Create Transfer Posting with Movement Type 541 to issue the subcomponents to the vendor
4. GR
5. IR

→ME21N → Enter Item Category L, Material (End Product), PO Quantity, Delivery Date, Net Price, Plant → Click on Item Details → Tab Material Data → Components, select Explode BOM → Click on Components button → Enter the subcomponents → Go back & Save.

Create Transfer Posting with movement type 541 & T Code MB1B
GR: MIGO
IR: MIRO

CONSIGNMENT: - (No Concept of Invoice)

In consignment process we will not create Purchasing document for the vendor, vendor himself send the material to our plant, though the material is available to our plant, the responsibility & ownership of the material is of vendor. A liability only arises when the material withdrawal (Consumption) is posted in the system from consignment stock.

Steps:

1. Create Consignment info record (mandatory)
2. Create Consignment purchase order with item category 'K' & maintain Info record number
3. Create GR Movement type '101K'
4. Create GI Movement Type '201K'
5. Consignment settlement T Code MRKO

→ ME11 → In info record →Purchasing Org Data 1 views of info record enter the tax code and save it

→ Create Consignment Purchase Order ME21N (Price option is grayed out with price zero)
→ Create GR with movement type 101K
→ Create Goods Issue (GI) T Code MB1A & Movement Type 201K → Enter Cost center vendor
→Consignment Settlement T Code MRKO → Click Activate Consignment → Activate Settle → Execute
Display the Document Number i.e. Invoice receipt T Code FB03

PIPELINE PROCESS: (No Concept of Invoice)

In pipeline handling your company does not need to order or store the material concerned. It is ready available to you as and when required via pipeline (e.g. oil or water), or some other type of cable (e.g. electricity). Consumption of the material is settled with the vendor on a regular basis.

Steps:
1. Create a Material master record with material type PIPE
2. Create Pipeline info record
3. Create GI with movement type 201P
4. Pipeline settlement T Code MRKO

RETURNABLE TRANSPORT PACKAGING (RTP):

When company orders goods from a vendor, the goods are delivered with returnable transport packaging (pallets, containers) that belongs to the vendor and is stored on our premises until you return it to the vendor.

Steps:
1. Create Material master record with material type LEIH
2. Create PO
3. Create GR by maintaining RTP material by selecting the option transport equipments with movement type 501M.
4. IR

STOCK TRANSFER:

In stock transfer processing, goods are procured and supplied within a company. One plant orders the goods internally to another plant (receiving plant/issuing plant). The goods are procured with a special type of purchase order - the stock transport order.

Steps:
1. Create a Material master in both supplying and receiving plant
2. Create stock transport order (STO) with item category 'U'
3. Create transfer posting with movement type **351** & T Code MB1B (Go to MMBE stock overview, the stock will decrease in supplying plant and it will not update stock of receiving plant, it will be under stock in transit)
4. Create GR stock will update in receiving plant

This scenario is under one company code between two plants.

THIRD - PARTY PROCESSING:

In third party processing, your company passes on a sales order to an external vendor who sends the goods directly to the customer. The sales order is not processed by your company, but by the vendor. Third-party items can be entered in purchase requisitions, purchase orders, and sales orders. Third party processing is integrated with Sales and Distribution. If the sales order contains third-party items, the system creates a purchase requisition from the order.

Steps:
1. Create MMR with sales views and maintain Division, Distribution channel, sales org. item category group and general item category group – BANS (Third party item) & Account group Sold to party
2. Create Customer master record T Code XD01, XD02, XD03
3. Create sales order T Code VA01, VA02, VA03 (PR generated automatically)
4. PO - T Code ME21N
5. GR – T Code MIGO
6. IR – T Code MIRO
7. Sales Billing / Billing Document T Code VF01, VF02, VF03

SPLIT VALUATION

Without split valuation, materials are valued at plant level. With split valuation, the same material number at a plant can have different stock quantity and value for different groupings (called valuation types).

The valuation types are set up in configuration could be for example:
- new, old or
- GB, US, AU, ... (indicating countries for example)
- Red, blue, black, etc.... (Indicating colors for example)

The valuation types are grouped together in a valuation category so for example, the above valuation types could be grouped by age, country, and color.

Entering the valuation type in the accounting view of the material master activates split valuation for the material

Valuation Category:

It determines how the material stocks are divided i.e. accounting to which criteria & indicates the characteristics of partial stocks.

Under valuation category we maintain valuation types

Valuation Type

It is a key that determines the split-valuated stocks of the material

Local definitions: It specifies to which plant the split valuation has maintained

IMPORTANT: It is only possible to change a material (valuation category) if no stock and PO were created. So it is not something that get changed at will. It needs to be decided on creation of material.

Steps to set it up

CONFIGURATION
1.   Activate Valuation in customization through T Code OMW0
2.   Create Valuation Category T Code OMWC
3.   Create Valuation Types T Code OMWC
4.   Link Categories > Types T Code OMWC
5.   Link valid Valuation Categories to Plant T Code OMWC

MASTER DATA
1.   Activate Split valuation for a material MM02
       (Add Valuation Category in material master in Accounting 1 view)
2.   Create Accounting views for every valuation type

Using Split Valuation in transactions
1.   Create Purchase Order
2.   Goods Receipt / Goods Issue
3.   Physical Inventory
4.   Stock Overview

In this example we want to group material in the same plant based on AGE (valuation category). We will have two "groups" (valuation types): OLD and NEW.

Configuration
SPRO →IMG→ Material Management > Valuation & A/C Assign > Split Valuation

1. Activate Valuation – T Code OMW0

Activate Valuation

Material valuation

⦿ Split material valuation active

◯ Split material valuation not active

2.Configure Split Valuation – T Code OMWC

Split Valuation of Materials

| Global types | Global categories | Local definitions |

3. Create Valuation Category

Select: Global Categories

Create Valuation Category

Create

Valuation Category   Y

Attributes

Description   AGE
Default:ext.procure.
☐   Ext.procurement mand
Default: in-house
☐   In-house prod. mand.
☐   Val. type automatic

The Ext Mandatory option will force users to enter a valuation type in purchase orders.
Select: Create (to save)

	Valuation Cat	DVT ExtPr	ExP	DVT InhPr	Inh	DVT Promo.	PrM	Autom.VTy
B	Inhse/Ext.Proc.	02	☑	01	☑		☐	☐
C	Status	C1	☐	C2	☐		☐	☐
H	Origin		☐		☐		☐	☐
R	Retail	RNORMAL	☐		☐	RAKTION	☐	☐
X	Automat.(Batch)		☐		☐		☐	☑
Y	AGE		☐		☐		☐	☐

4. Create Valuation Types

Select: Global Types > Create

Create Valuation Type

Create	Account cat. ref.

Valuation type	OLD

Attributes

Ext. purchase orders	2
Int. purchase orders	
Acct cat. reference	0001

Select: Create (to save)

The Purchase Orders attributes option indicate if PO's are allowed or not.
1 - Not allowed
2 - Allowed but with warning
3 - Allowed

The account category reference determines what GL valuation classes will be allowed.

4. Link Categories > Types

Select: Global categories (from main config menu)
Select: Valuation Category
Select: Types > cat.

Global Valuation Categories

		Create	Change	Delete	Types -> cat.

Valuation Cat.		DVT ExtPr	ExP	DVT InhPr	Inh	DVT Promo.	PrM	Autom.VTy
B	Inhse/Ext.Proc.	02	✓	01	✓			
C	Status	C1		C2				
H	Origin							
R	Retail	RNORMAL				RAKTION		
X	Automat.(Batch)							✓
Y	AGE							
Z	STATUS							

Activate valid valuation categories

Valuation Cat.		Y	AGE	

Assignment						
Status	Valuation type		Ex	In	ARef	De
	01		0	2	0001	Re
	02		2	0	0001	Re
	C1		2	2	0003	Go
	C2		2	2	0003	Go
	C3		2	2	0003	Go
	EIGEN		0	2	0001	Re
	FREMD		2	0	0001	Re
	LAND 1		2	0	0001	Re
	LAND 2		2	0	0001	Re
Active	NEW		2		0003	Go
Active	OLD		2		0003	Go
	RAKTION		2	2	0005	Re
	RNORMAL		2	2	0005	Re

Activate		Deactivate

5. Link valid Valuation Categories to Plant

Select: Local Definitions (from main config menu)
Select: Plant to use
Select: Cats -> OU
Select: Valuation Category and press Activate

| Local types | Local categories |

Allocation of Valuation Categories

Status		Valuation Cat.	DVT ExtPr	ExP	DVT InhPr	Inh	DVT Promo.	PrM	VT
	B	Inhse/Ext.Proc.	02	✓	01	✓		☐	☐
	C	Status	C1	☐	C2	☐		☐	☐
	H	Origin		☐		☐		☐	☐
	R	Retail	RNORMAL	☐		☐	RAKTION	☐	☐
	X	Automat.(Batch)		☐		☐		☐	✓
Active	N	GE		☐		☐		☐	☐
Active	Z	STATUS		☐		☐		☐	☐

| Activate | Deactivate | Entry 1 of 7 |

ACTIVATE MATERIAL MASTER

1. Activate Split valuation for a material

(Add Valuation Category in material master)
Material Master create - MM01

| 2 | Accounting 1 | Accounting 2 | | ◀ ▶ |

Spare Parts

EA	each	Valuation Category	Y
		Current Period	06 2006
		Price determ.	☐ ML act.

NOTE: It is only possible to change a material (valuation category) if no stock and PO were created. So it is not something that gets changed at will. It needs to be decided on creation of material.

2. Create Accounting views for every valuation type - mm01

Create Material (Initial Screen)

Select view(s)   Organizational levels   Data

Material
Industry sector
Material type

Change Number

Copy from...
Material

Organizational Levels

Organizational levels

Plant   1000

Valuation type   NEW

☐ Org. levels/profiles only on request

✓ Select view(s)   🖫 Default values   ✂

Plant data / stor. 2   Accounting 1   Accounting 2

Material   310   Spare Parts
Plant   1000
Val. type   NEW

General data

Base Unit of Measure   EA   each   Valuation Category   Y
Currency   ᐟᵀᴬᵢᐟ   Current Period   06 2006
Division   Price determ.   ☐ ML act.

Current valuation

Valuation Class
VC: Sales order stk   Proj. stk val. class
Price control   V   Price unit   1
Moving price   Standard price
Total stock   0   Total value   0.00
                                           ☐ Valuated Un
Future price   Valid from

Previous period/year   Std cost estimate

USING SPLIT VALUATION IN TRANSACTIONS

1. Create Purchase Order - ME21N

2. Goods Receipt / Goods Issue – MIGO

4. Physical Inventory - example MI10

Note that the batch field is used!

5. **Stock Overview** – MMBE

Stock Overview: Basic List

Selection

Material	000000000000000310	Spare Parts	
Matl Type			
Unit of Meas.	EA	Base Unit of Meas.	EA

Stock Overview

Detailed Display

Client/Company Code/Plant/Storage Location/Batch/Special Stock	Unrestricted use
Total	1,000.000
	1,000.000
	1,000.000
	1,000.000
NEW	1,000.000

AUOTOMATIC ACCOUNT DETERMINATION OR ASSIGNMENT

Whenever there is goods movement accounting documents/ financial accounts updated automatically, so we do some settings in customization is called automatic account assignment.

It works with three important factors: -
- Chart of accounts
- Material type
- Valuation grouping code

Chart of accounts: - It is a group of accounts (GL Accounts), which is assigned to our company code. One company code is assigned to one chart of account but one chart of account can be maintained for n number of company codes.

Valuation grouping code / valuation modification: - It is a 4-digit code, which is assigned to company code along with valuation area (Plant)

Account category reference: - It is a 4-digit code that establishes relationship between material types and valuation class. One account cat ref assigned to n number of material type and valuation class

Transaction / Event key: - It is an internal processing key that facilitates the automatic account determination for the various material and invoice posting.
Use: - Key to determine the account in which a posting line is generated (at least two transaction event keys are involved in each posting)

Value String: - It indicates the posting rule that always contain same account assignment char to certain transaction / event key

Account Modifier: - It is a subdivision of transaction event key in which GL account is linked during the process of automatic account determination.
Valuation class and material type is assigned to it

Steps: -
1. Activate valuation Group code
2. Assign Valuation area to valuation grouping code
3. Create Account Cat Ref and valuation class
4. Assign valuation class to Account Cat Ref
5. Assign Account Cat Ref to Material type
6. Assign account grouping to movement types
7. Configure Automatic posting

Customize settings

SPRO → IMG → MM → Valuation Class and Account Assignment → Account Determination → Account determination without wizard

1. Define valuation control T Code OMWM
2. Group together valuation areas T Code OMWD
3. Define valuation class T Code OMSK
   - Account category reference
   - Valuation class
   - Material type / Account Cat Ref
4. Define Account grouping for movement type T Code OMWN
5. Configure automatic posting T Code OMWB

Transaction/ Event Key's

BSX	-	Stock Posting / Inventory Posting
PRD	-	Price difference
GBB	-	Offsetting entry for stock posting
WRX	-	GR/IR Clearing
FRI	-	Freight Clearing

LSMW (LEGACY SYSTEM MIGRATION WORKBENCH)

Legacy System Migration Workbench or LSMW is SAP standard program that can be used to easily load / change master data or transactions in SAP without any programming at all. It can be used to upload data at cutover, such as: open orders, contracts, materials, vendors, stock on hand, It can also be used in a production system to make changes to existing data. Very limited authorisation checks are available on the transaction, so the use of it must be very well controlled.

Below is a simple example where vendor masters are loaded using recording in LSMW.

In our example, we will follow these steps.
- Start program and create a project
- Record the transaction to be used in the load
- Define the fields to be loaded
- Define conversion rules to take place
- Define the file name
- Upload the file from PC to SAP
- Convert to correct format
- Create and run batch input session

Start it all by executing transaction LSWM (program /SAPDMC/SAPMLSMW). Define Project / subproject / Object. It is also possible to export the project to a text file, to be imported into another system.

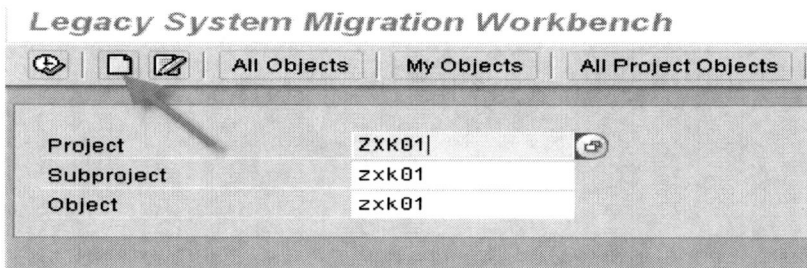

Various methods can be used to load the file (BAPI, ALE, recording ....). We will be using a recorded transaction. To record the transaction, we give the recording a name and type in the transaction code that will be used.

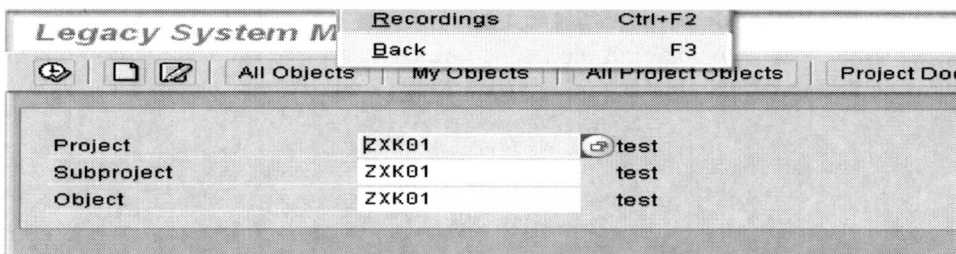

Recordings of Project 'ZXK01': Overview

☐ ✎ ✂ ⧉ ▷▷ 🗑 ⊷ ⊞ ⊟ ⊞ Subtree ⊞ Row

Create Recording

Recording	zxk01
Description	vendor
Owner	SAP123

✓ ✗

Transaction Code ☒

Transaction Code   xk01

✓ ✗

Step through the screens as you would have done it manually.

Create Vendor: Initial Screen

Vendor	A100
Company Code	
Purch. organization	
Account group	LIEF

Reference

Vendor	
Company code	
Purch. organization	

☐ Use central address management

Create Vendor: Address

💾 📋 🈁 CIN Details

Vendor	A100

Address

Title			
Name	SAP123.com	Search term	SAP123
Street		PO Box	
City	London	Postal Code	
District			
P.O.Box city		PO Box PCode	
Country	GB	Region	

A screen will be shown with all the fields that were recorded. Every field needs a name. To keep it simple, allocate the default SAP name to the fields. Make sure all the fields you want to load/change are in the list. If not, re-record the transaction and ensure you do a dropdown or type in values in the correct field.

```
Create Recording
Default  Default All  Reset  | Screen Field  Screen Field  |  | Repeat Recording  Maintain Attributes  |

Recording ZXK01              test
     └─ XK01 Create vendor (centrally)
          └─ SAPMF02K 0100
               ├─── BDC_CURSOR        T077Y-TXT30
               ├─── BDC_OKCODE        /00
               ├─── RF02K-LIFNR       A100          LIFNR      Vendor Account Number
               └─── RF02K-KTOKK       LIEF          KTOKK      Vendor account group
          └─ SAPMF02K 0110
               ├─── BDC_CURSOR        LFA1-SPRAS
               ├─── BDC_OKCODE        =UPDA
               ├─── LFA1-NAME1        SAP123.com    NAME1      Name 1
               ├─── LFA1-SORTL        SAP123        SORTL      Sort field
               ├─── LFA1-ORT01        London        ORT01      City
               ├─── LFA1-LAND1        GB            LAND1      Country Key
               ├─── LFA1-SPRAS        EN            SPRAS      Language Key
               └─── LFA1-PSTLZ        1234          PSTLZ      Postal Code
```

Recordings of Project 'ZXK01': Overview

```
 🗋 🖉 ✂ 🗐 ▷▷ 🗑 ⇗ 🖭 🖷 🗐 Subtree  🗐 Row

Recordings
   ├── ZXK01       test
                   Transaction:        XK01 Create vendor (centrally)
```

Legacy System Migration Workb

```
 ⊕ | 🗋 📝 |  All Objects  |  My Objects  | /

Project      ZXK01
Subproject   ZXK01
Object       ZXK01
```

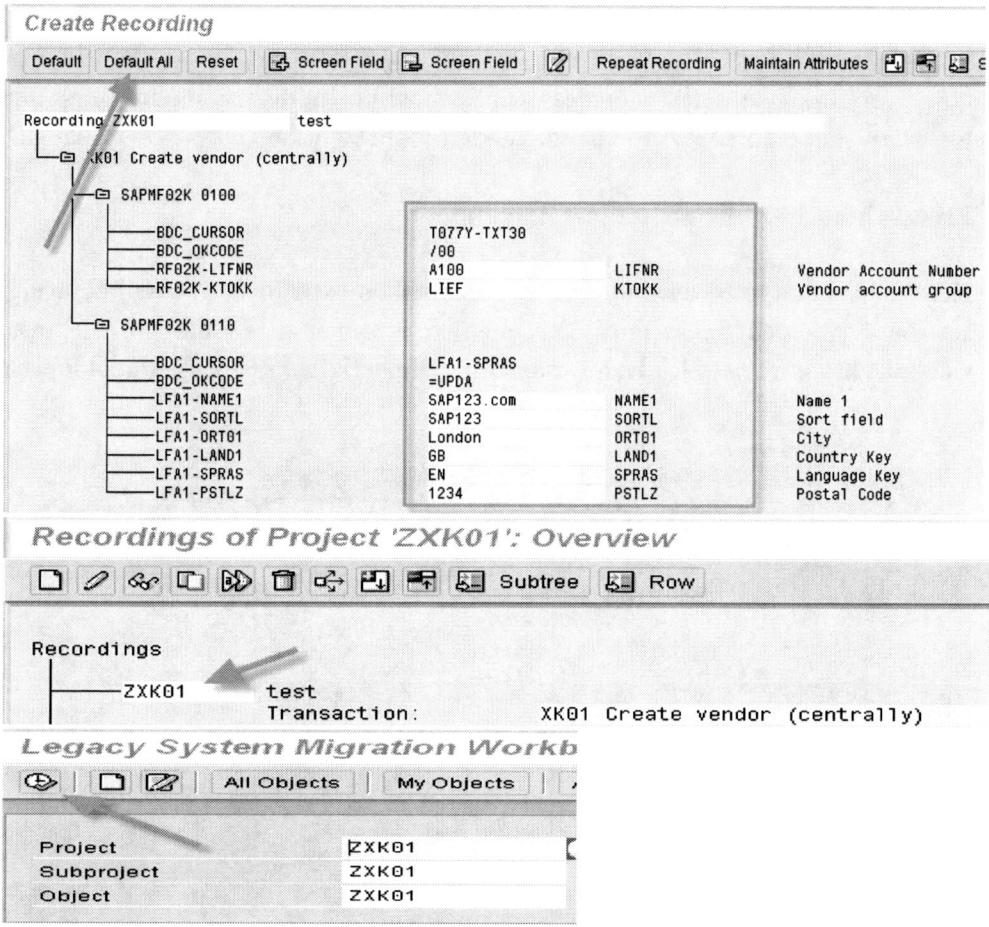

Here is a list of all the process steps that available. In our example, not all will be used. Those to be used in example are mark with a red dot. So, we will be using Process Step 1, 3, 4, 5, 7, 8, 9, 11, 12, 13.

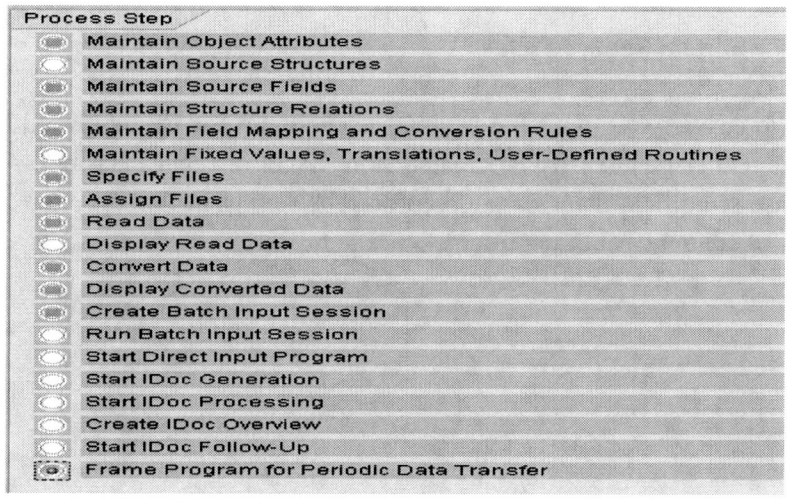

```
Process Step
  (●)  Maintain Object Attributes
  ( )  Maintain Source Structures
  (●)  Maintain Source Fields
  (●)  Maintain Structure Relations
  (●)  Maintain Field Mapping and Conversion Rules
  ( )  Maintain Fixed Values, Translations, User-Defined Routines
  (●)  Specify Files
  (●)  Assign Files
  (●)  Read Data
  (●)  Display Read Data
  (●)  Convert Data
  (●)  Display Converted Data
  (●)  Create Batch Input Session
  ( )  Run Batch Input Session
  ( )  Start Direct Input Program
  ( )  Start IDoc Generation
  ( )  Start IDoc Processing
  ( )  Create IDoc Overview
  ( )  Start IDoc Follow-Up
  (◉)  Frame Program for Periodic Data Transfer
```

The next screens are the process steps as in screen above.

NB: Every time you select a process step, you will be in display mode -- first thing to do for every step is to switch to change mode by clicking the "Display<->Change" button.

Process Step 1 - Maintain Object Attributes

Here the method to be used to load the information is defined. We will be using a BDC session / recorded transaction. This method is quick to do but not the fastest. For example, if you want to load a huge amount of materials, anthers use direct input method.

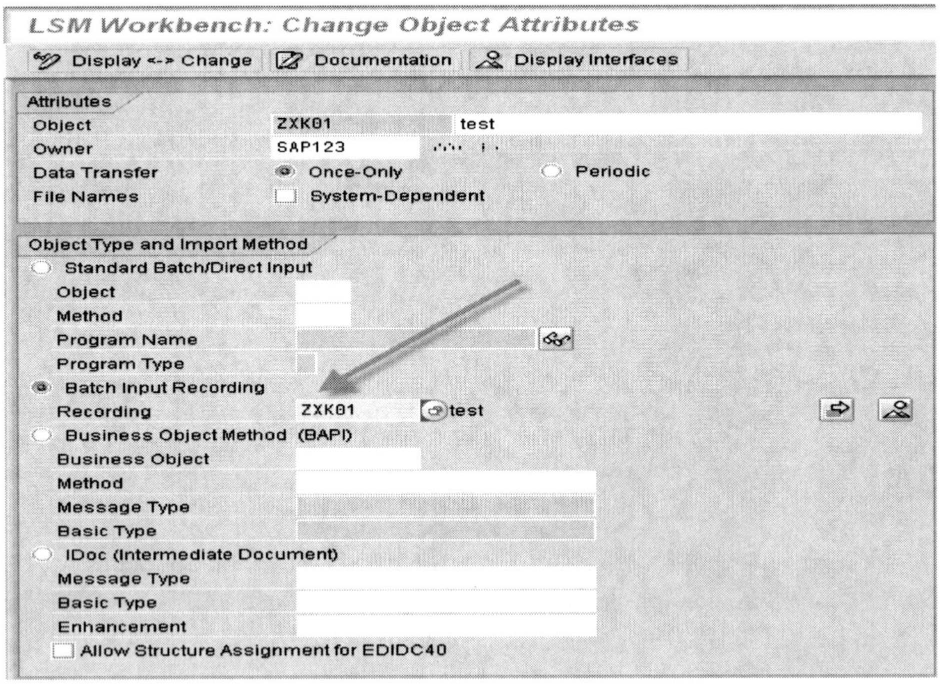

Process Step 3 - Maintain Source Fields

The next step is to ensure your input file is created. The input file (to be loaded in SAP) is a text file. The text file can easily be created from Excel or other data tool. Again to keep it simple, use same field names as in recording. A setting in Process Step XX will ensure that order of columns is not important.

As can be seen – in our case we used comma delimited text. It is generally better to use tab delimited format to avoid errors (example where text fields may contain commas). If you will be using LSMW quite a lot, it is better to get a better text editor and not used Notepad (as shown in screen below).

Back in LSMW, the fields in external file is defined, so make them the same as in txt file.

Process Step 4 - Maintain Structure Relationship

Link between recorded fields and external fields.

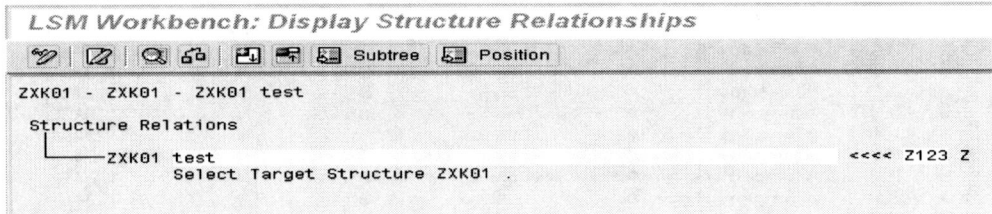

```
LSM Workbench: Display Structure Relationships
 🗞  🖉  🔍 🔊  🖅 🖅 🖳 Subtree  🖳 Position

ZXK01 - ZXK01 - ZXK01 test

 Structure Relations
   └──────ZXK01 test                                              <<<< Z123 Z
              Select Target Structure ZXK01 .
```

Process Step 5 - Maintain Field Mapping and Conversion Rules

In this step the rule on where the value of the recorded fields will come from is specified. Example: values can come from an external file or a constant can be defined (for fields that will not change).

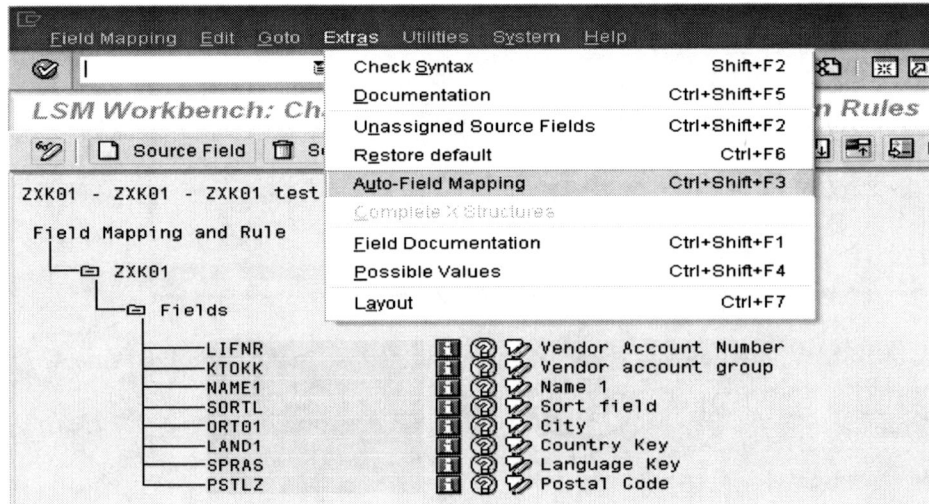

```
  Field Mapping  Edit  Goto  Extras  Utilities  System  Help
 ✓  I              ⌐  Check Syntax              Shift+F2       🗗  🔀 ⌑
                      Documentation             Ctrl+Shift+F5
 LSM Workbench: Ch    Unassigned Source Fields  Ctrl+Shift+F2    Rules
 🗞  🗋 Source Field 🗑 S Restore default            Ctrl+F6    🖳 🖅 🖳 F
                      Auto-Field Mapping        Ctrl+Shift+F3
ZXK01 - ZXK01 - ZXK01 test   Complete X Structures
                      Field Documentation       Ctrl+Shift+F1
Field Mapping and Rule Possible Values          Ctrl+Shift+F4
   └─🖿 ZXK01           Layout                       Ctrl+F7
      └─🖿 Fields
            ├──LIFNR           🔢 ⑦ 🖘 Vendor Account Number
            ├──KTOKK           🔢 ⑦ 🖘 Vendor account group
            ├──NAME1           🔢 ⑦ 🖘 Name 1
            ├──SORTL           🔢 ⑦ 🖘 Sort field
            ├──ORT01           🔢 ⑦ 🖘 City
            ├──LAND1           🔢 ⑦ 🖘 Country Key
            ├──SPRAS           🔢 ⑦ 🖘 Language Key
            └──PSTLZ           🔢 ⑦ 🖘 Postal Code
```

Auto Field Mapping: Settings

- ◉ Edit All Target Fields
- ○ Edit All Target Fields from Cursor Position

- ◉ Only Edit Initial Target Fields
- ○ Also Edit Non-Initial Target Fields

- ◉ Match Fields with the Same Name
- ○ Match Fields with Similar Names
  - Fuzzy Probability in Percent | 50

- ◉ Only Apply Rule "Transfer (MOVE)"
- ○ Also Apply Reusable Rules

- ☐ Only If Source Field Not Initial

- ○ With Confirmation
- ◉ No Confirmation

✓ ✗

LSM Workbench: Change Field Mapping and Conversion Rules

✎ | ☐ Source Field | 🗑 Source Field | 🏗 Rule | 📝 | 🔧 🔧 🔲 ⑦ | 📄 📑 🔲 Position

```
ZXK01 - ZXK01 - ZXK01 test

Field Mapping and Rule                    ✎
   └─ 🗀 ZXK01                            test
        └─ 🗀 Fields
             ├── LIFNR          🔲 ⑦ ✎ Vendor Account Number
             │                  Source:  Z123-LIFNR ()
             │                  Rule :   Transfer (MOVE)
             │                  Code:    ZXK01-LIFNR = Z123-LIFNR.
             │                           * Caution: Source field is longer than ta
             ├── KTOKK          🔲 ⑦ ✎ Vendor account group
             ├── NAME1          🔲 ⑦ ✎ Name 1
             │                  Source:  Z123-NAME1 ()
             │                  Rule :   Transfer (MOVE)
             │                  Code:    ZXK01-NAME1 = Z123-NAME1.
             │                           * Caution: Source field is longer than ta
             ├── SORTL          🔲 ⑦ ✎ Sort field
             │                  Source:  Z123-SORTL ()
             │                  Rule :   Transfer (MOVE)
             │                  Code:    ZXK01-SORTL = Z123-SORTL.
             │                           * Caution: Source field is longer than ta
             ├── ORT01          🔲 ⑦ ✎ City
             │                  Source:  Z123-ORT01 ()
             │                  Rule :   Transfer (MOVE)
             │                  Code:    ZXK01-ORT01 = Z123-ORT01.
             │                           * Caution: Source field is longer than ta
             ├── LAND1          🔲 ⑦ ✎ Country Key
             │                  Source:  Z123-LAND1 ()
             │                  Rule :   Transfer (MOVE)
             │                  Code:    ZXK01-LAND1 = Z123-LAND1.
             │                           * Caution: Source field is longer than ta
             ├── SPRAS          🔲 ⑦ ✎ Language Key
             │                  Source:  Z123-SPRAS
```

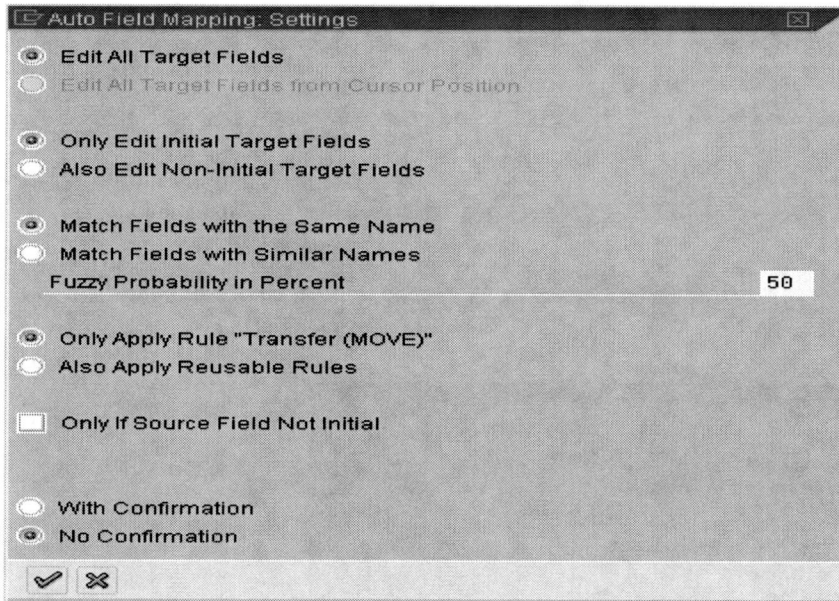

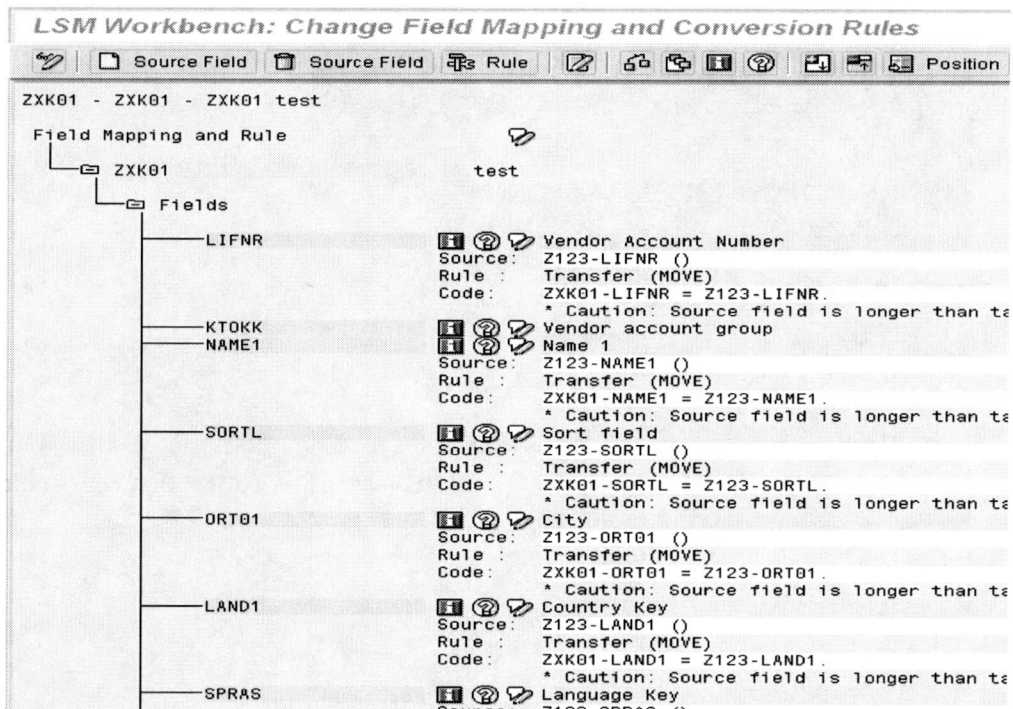

Vendor account group will not be read from external file. Let's make the field a constant value of LIEF.

```
       ~     |  □ Source Field |  🗍 Source Field  | 🎏 Rule  |  ☑ | 🔁 🔁 🔳 ⑳ | 🖳 🖳

ZXK01 - ZXK01 - ZXK01 test

Field Mapping and Rule                    🤚

       └──🖻 ZXK01                       test

              └──🖻 Fields

                      ──LIFNR          🔳 ⑳ 🤚 Vendor Account Number
                                       Source: Z123-LIFNR ()
                                       Rule :  Transfer (MOVE)
                                       Code:   ZXK01-LIFNR = Z123-LIFNR.
                                        * Caution: Source field is lor
                      ──KTOKK           🔳 ⑳ 🤚 Vendor account group
                      ──NAME1           🔳 ⑳ 🤚 Name 1
                                       Source: Z123-NAME1 ()
```

```
┌─ ZXK01-KTOKK: Choose Rule ──────────────────────────┬─┐
│                                                      ⊠ │
│  ○  Initial                                            │
│ ┌──────────────────────────────────────────────────┐  │
│ │○  Constant                                         │  │
│ └──────────────────────────────────────────────────┘  │
│  ○  Transfer (MOVE)                                    │
│  ○  Fixed Value (Reusable)                             │
│  ○  Translation (Reusable)                             │
│  ○  Prefix                                             │
│  ○  Suffix                                             │
│  ○  Concatenation                                      │
│  ○  Transfer Left-Aligned                              │
│  ○  ABAP Code                                          │
│  ○  User-Defined Routine (Reusable)                    │
│  ○  X FIELD                                            │
│  ○  Move With Leading Zeros                            │
│                                                        │
│  ☐  Only If Source Field Not Initial                   │
│                                                        │
│  ✓  ✖                                                  │
└────────────────────────────────────────────────────────┘
```

```
┌─ Value For ZXK01-KTOKK ──────────────┬─┐
│                                      ⊠ │
│  Account group          LIEF  ⊕       │
│                                        │
│  ✓  ✖                                  │
└──────────────────────────────────────┘
```

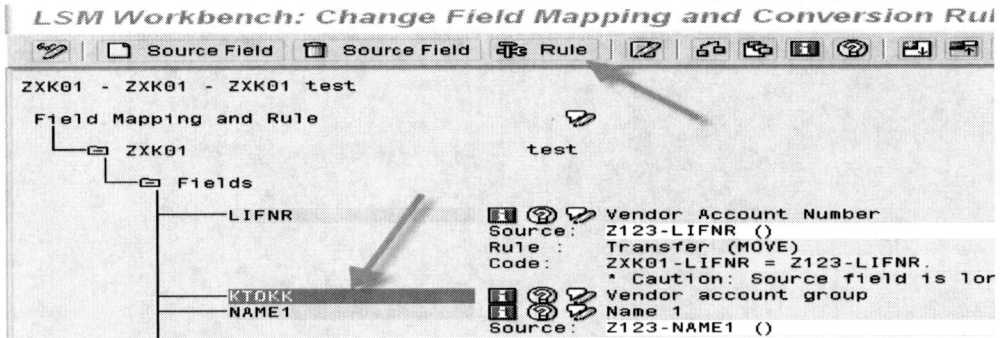

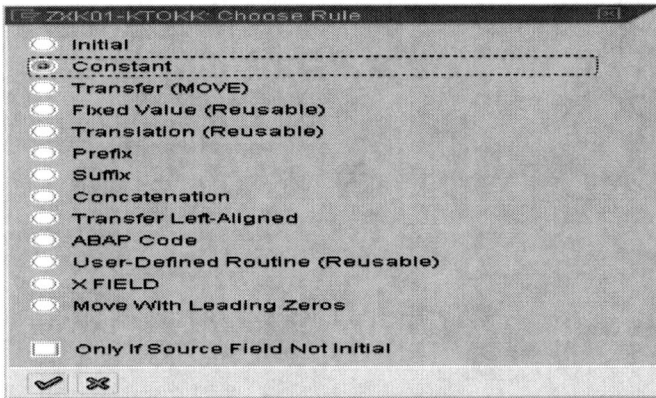

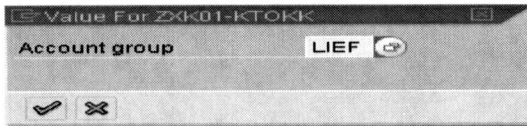

Process Step 7 - Specify Files

Before loading the file from PC, one specifies the structure. In this case comma delimited were used (although, tab delimited are more common). Also the first row contains the header.

File on Front End: Maintain Properties

File   C:\lsmw\vendors.txt

Name   zvendors

File Contents
- ⦿ Data for One Source Structure (Table)
- ○ Data for Multiple Source Structures (Seq. File)

Delimiter
- ○ No Separator   →   ⦿ Comma
- ○ Tabulator   ○ Blanks
- ○ Semi-Colon   ○ Other

File Structure
- ☑ Field Names at Start of File
- ☐ Field Order Matches Source Structure Definition

File Type
- ⦿ Record End Marker (Text File)
- ○ Fixed Rec. Length (Bin.File)
- ○ Hexadecimal Lth Field (4 Bytes) at Start of Record

Code Page
- ⦿ ASCII   ○ IBM DOS

✓ ✗

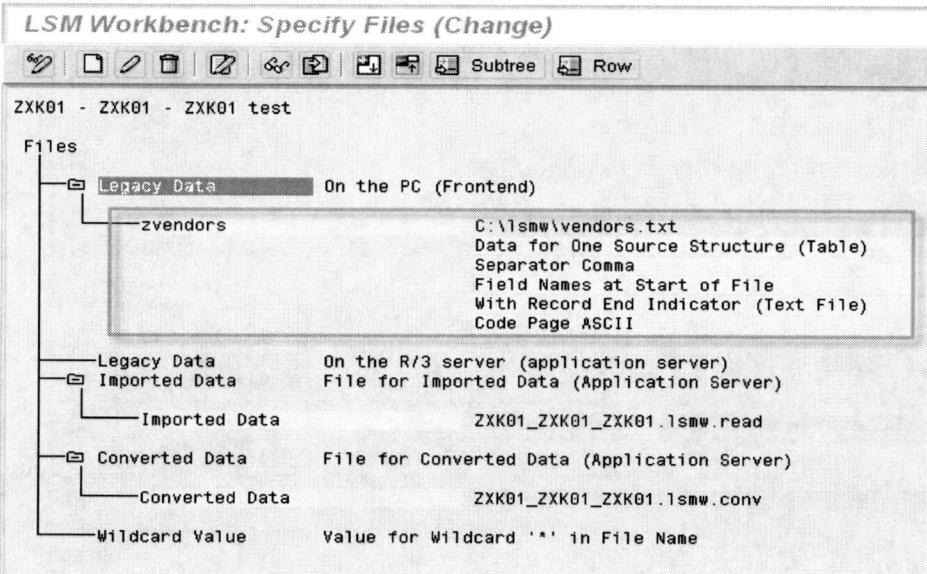

```
LSM Workbench: Specify Files (Change)

ZXK01 - ZXK01 - ZXK01 test

Files
  └─ Legacy Data          On the PC (Frontend)
       └─ zvendors                    C:\lsmw\vendors.txt
                                      Data for One Source Structure (Table)
                                      Separator Comma
                                      Field Names at Start of File
                                      With Record End Indicator (Text File)
                                      Code Page ASCII
     ── Legacy Data        On the R/3 server (application server)
  └─ Imported Data         File for Imported Data (Application Server)
       └─ Imported Data              ZXK01_ZXK01_ZXK01.lsmw.read
  └─ Converted Data        File for Converted Data (Application Server)
       └─ Converted Data             ZXK01_ZXK01_ZXK01.lsmw.conv
     ── Wildcard Value      Value for Wildcard '*' in File Name
```

Process Step 9 - Read Data

Load the file into SAP from your PC.

```
LSM Workbench: Import Data For ZXK01, ZXK01, ZXK01

19.12.2005 - 12:18:38

File(s) Read:        C:\lsmw\vendors.txt
File Written:        ZXK01_ZXK01_ZXK01.lsmw.read

Source Structure           Read      Written      Not Written

Z123                         10         10             0

Transactions Read:              10
Records Read:                   10
Transactions Written:           10
Records Written:                10
```

Process Step 11 - Convert Data

This applies the conversion rules that was set up in Process Step 5. So after this, all the fields to be loaded must be present and all rules applied.

```
LSM Workbench: Convert Data For ZXK01, ZXK01, ZXK01

19.12.2005 - 12:19:47

File Read:           ZXK01_ZXK01_ZXK01.lsmw.read
File Written:        ZXK01_ZXK01_ZXK01.lsmw.conv

Transactions Read:              10
Records Read:                   10
Transactions Written:           10
Records Written:                10
```

Process Step 12 - Display Converted Data

It is a good idea at this stage to view a sample set of the data to ensure that everything is ok.

```
LSM Workbench: Converted Data

 Field Contents    Change Display    Display Colour Legend

File  ZXK01_ZXK01_ZXK01.lsmw.conv

Row     Structur                          Contents

    1  ZXK01                            ZXK01
    2  ZXK01                            ZXK01
    3  ZXK01                            ZXK01
    4  ZXK01                            ZXK01
    5  ZXK01                            ZXK01
    6  ZXK01                            ZXK01
    7  ZXK01                            ZXK01
    8  ZXK01                            ZXK01
    9  ZXK01                            ZXK01
   10  ZXK01                            ZXK01
```

LSM Workbench: Converted Data

Fld Name	Fld Text	FldValue
File	ZXK01_ZXK01_ZXK01.lsmw.conv	
Structure	ZXK01	
TABNAME	Table Name	ZXK01
TCODE	Transaction Code	XK01
LIFNR	Vendor Account Number	A106
KTOKK	Vendor account group	LIEF
NAME1	Name 1	Company F
SORTL	Sort field	A
ORT01	City	Manchester
LAND1	Country Key	GB
SPRAS	Language Key	EN
PSTLZ	Postal Code	12345

Process Step 13 - Create Batch Input Session

Generate a batch input session

LSM Workbench: Generate Batch Input Folder

File Name (with Path)	ZXK01_ZXK01_ZXK01.lsmw.conv
Display Trans. per BI Folder	
Name of Batch Input Folder(s)	ZXK01
User ID	SAP123
☐ Keep batch input folder(s)?	

Information

ⓘ 1 batch input folder with 10 transactions created

And process the batch input session.

Batch Input: Session Overview

🖪 Analysis ⊕ Process 🖪 Statistics 🖺 Log 🖺 Recording

Selection criteria

Sess.: ZXK01   From: To: Created by: *

| New | Incorrect | Processed | In Process | In Background | Being Created | Locked |

Session name	Sta...	Date	Time	Creation Program	Lock Date	Σ Trans.	◑	⊘	Σ Screens	D.	Que
ZXK01	🗋	19.12.2005	12:24:21	/SAPDMC/SAP_LSM..		10	0	0	20	✓	051

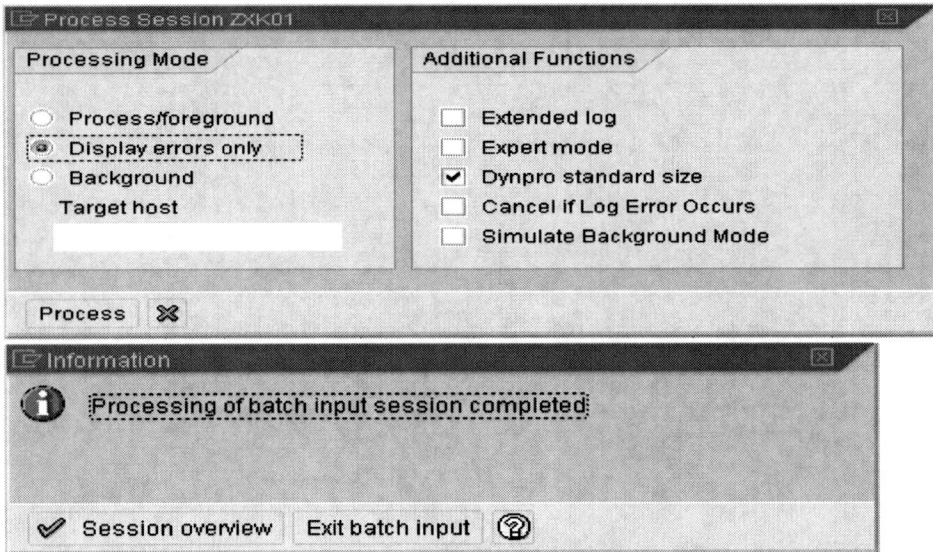

You are done!

To confirm that the data was loaded correctly, verify that vendors were loaded correctly.

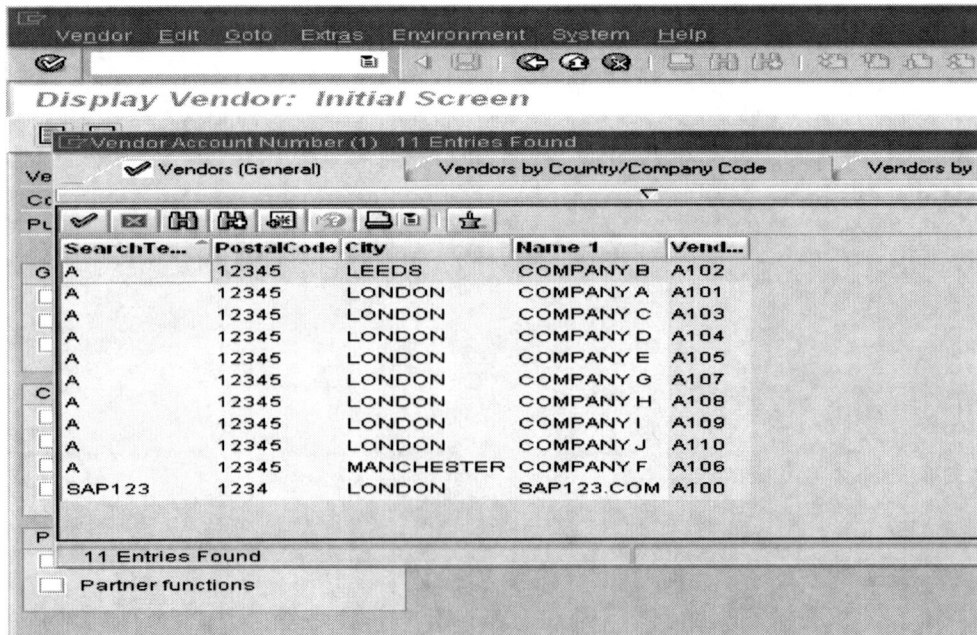

IMPORTANT TABLES IS SAP MM

EINA	Purchasing Info Record- General Data
EINE	Purchasing Info Record- Purchasing Organization Data
MAKT	Material Descriptions
MARA	General Material Data
MARC	Plant Data for Material
MARD	Storage Location Data for Material
MAST	Material to BOM Link
MBEW	Material Valuation
MKPF	Header- Material Document
MSEG	Document Segment- Material
MVER	Material Consumption
MVKE	Sales Data for materials
RKPF	Document Header- Reservation
T023	Mat. groups
T024	Purchasing Groups
T156	Movement Type
T157H	Help Texts for Movement Types
MOFF	Lists what views have not been created
A501	Plant/Material
EBAN	Purchase Requisition
EBKN	Purchase Requisition Account Assignment
EKAB	Release Documentation
EKBE	History per Purchasing Document
EKET	Scheduling Agreement Schedule Lines
EKKN	Account Assignment in Purchasing Document
EKKO	Purchasing Document Header
EKPO	Purchasing Document Item
IKPF	Header- Physical Inventory Document
ISEG	Physical Inventory Document Items
LFA1	Vendor Master (General section)
LFB1	Vendor Master (Company Code)
NRIV	Number range intervals
RESB	Reservation/dependent requirements
T161T	Texts for Purchasing Document Types

FACTORY CALENDAR

A factory calendar distinguishes between working days and non-working days.

If you have entered an exception rule for non-working days and have selected factory calendar, you must enter a factory calendar that is relevant to your company.
T.CODE: - OY05
PATH: -

SPRO → IMG → Time Management → Work Schedules → Define Public Holiday Classes

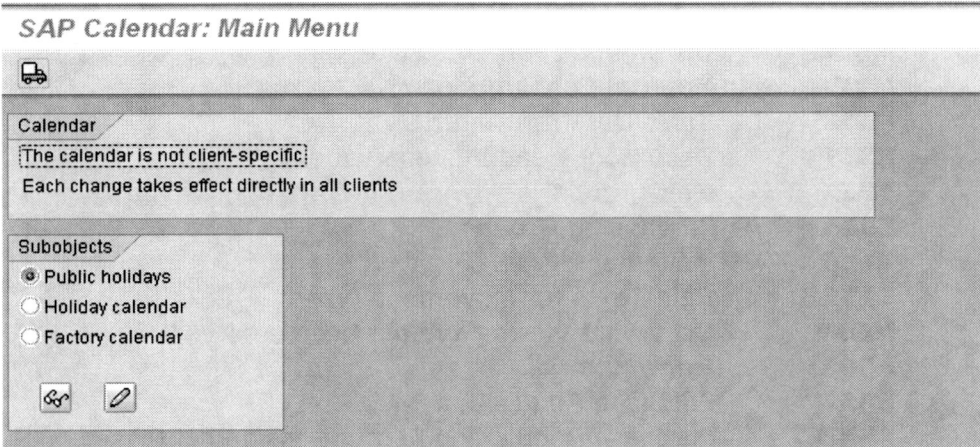

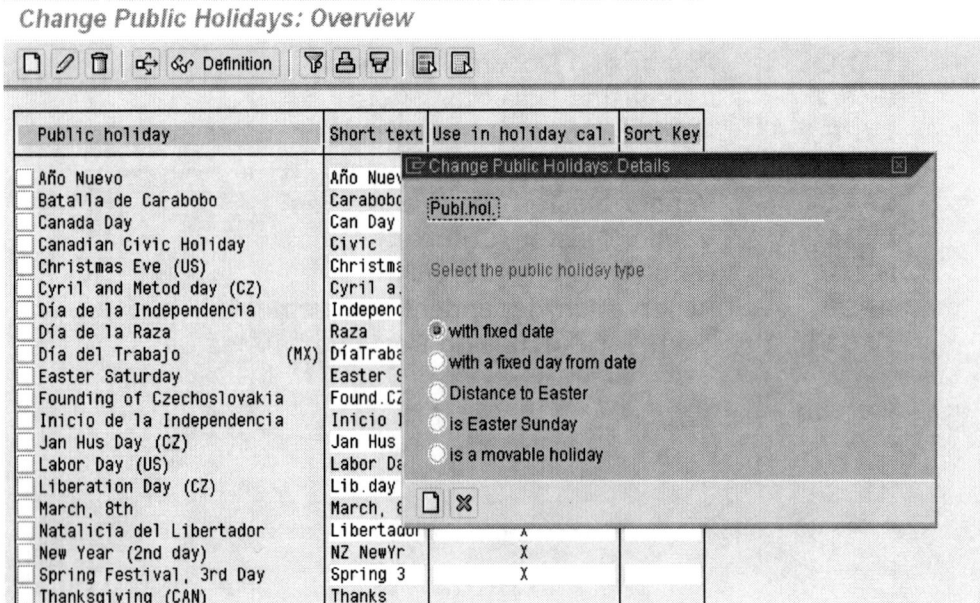

SAP Calendar: Main Menu

Calendar

The calendar is not client-specific

Each change takes effect directly in all clients

Subobjects
- ● Public holidays
- ○ Holiday calendar
- ○ Factory calendar

Change Public Holidays: Overview

Public holiday	Short text	Use in holiday cal.	Sort Key
Año Nuevo	Año Nuev		
Batalla de Carabobo	Carabobo		
Canada Day	Can Day		
Canadian Civic Holiday	Civic		
Christmas Eve (US)	Christma		
Cyril and Metod day (CZ)	Cyril a.		
Día de la Independencia	Independ		
Día de la Raza	Raza		
Día del Trabajo (MX)	DíaTraba		
Easter Saturday	Easter S		
Founding of Czechoslovakia	Found.Cz		
Inicio de la Independencia	Inicio I		
Jan Hus Day (CZ)	Jan Hus		
Labor Day (US)	Labor Da		
Liberation Day (CZ)	Lib.day		
March, 8th	March, 8		
Natalicia del Libertador	Libertador	X	
New Year (2nd day)	NZ NewYr	X	
Spring Festival, 3rd Day	Spring 3	X	
Thanksgiving (CAN)	Thanks		

Change Public Holidays: Details

Publ.hol.

Select the public holiday type

- ● with fixed date
- ○ with a fixed day from date
- ○ Distance to Easter
- ○ is Easter Sunday
- ○ is a movable holiday

Change Public Holidays: Overview

🗋 🖉 🗑 🖧 ᘒ Definition ⏐ ᘒ 🖨 ᘒ ⏐ 🖳 🖳

Public holiday	Short text	Use in holiday cal.	Sort Key

⌐ Change Public Holidays: Details ⏐ ⌐ Change Public Holidays: Fixed Dates ⏐ ⊠

Public holiday definition

Day	15
Month	8

Guaranteed

- ◉ Not guaranteed
- ○ Thursday
- ○ Friday
- ○ Sunday
- ○ Saturday/Sunday

Public holiday attributes

Sort criterion	099
Religion	Hindu
Holiday class	
Public holidays shrt	INDEPEND
Holidays long text	INDEPENDENCE DAY (INDIA)

🖉 ✖

Whit Sunday	Whit Sun.	X	080

SAP Calendar: Main Menu

🖴

Calendar

The calendar is not client-specific

Each change takes effect directly in all clients

Subobjects

- ○ Public holidays
- ◉ Holiday calendar
- ○ Factory calendar

🖧 🖉

Change Public Holiday Calendar: Details

◀ Calendar ▶ Calendar ▣ ▣

| Calendar ID | 88 VYASENTERPRISE |

Valid Fr.year 2008
       To year 2012

Public holidays assigned

| Public Holiday | Valid from | Valid to |

Entry   0   of   0

| Assign publ.holiday | Delete Assignment |

Change Public Holiday Calendar: Details

◀ Calendar ▶ Calendar ▣ ▣

| Calendar ID | 88 VYASENTERPRISE |

Valid Fr.year 2008
       To year

Public holidays ass

Public Holida

Insert Public Holidays into Holiday Calendar ☒

Public holiday	Key
☐ New Year's Day	010
☐ Epiphany	020
☐ St. Joseph	025
☐ Maundy Thursday	028
☐ Green Thursday	029
☐ Good Friday	030
☐ Easter Sunday	040
☐ Easter Monday	050
☐ May Day	060
☐ Ascension	070
☐ Whit Sunday	080
☐ Whit Monday	090
☑ INDEPENDENCE DAY (INDIA)	099
☑ JANMASTMI	099
☑ Rakshabandhan	099
☐ Corpus Christi	100
☐ Assumption	120
☐ Foundation day of Bike Interna	130
☐ All Saints' Day	150

Assign publ.holiday ▽ ᗺ ▽ ▣ ▣ ▣ ▥ ▦ ✖

SAP Calendar: Main Menu

🖶

Calendar

The calendar is not client-specific

Each change takes effect directly in all clients

Subobjects

◯ Public holidays
◯ Holiday calendar
◉ Factory calendar

👓 ✏️

Change Factory Calendar: Details

| Special rules | ◀ Calendar | ▶ Calendar | 🔳 🔳 |

Factory Cal.ID   99 FACTORY CALENDAR OF INDIA

Valid   Fr.year   2008
           To year   2008

Holiday cal. ID   88 VYAS ENTERPRISE

Special rules   none exist

No. first workday   _____

Workdays

☑ Monday
☑ Tuesday
☑ Wednesday
☑ Thursday
☑ Friday
☑ Saturday
☑ Sunday
☐ Public holiday

MATERIAL MANAGEMENT / PROCUREMENT PROCESS

The typical procurement cycle for a service or material consists of the following phases,

1. **Determination of Requirements :-**
   Materials requirement are identified either in the user departments or via materials planning and control. You can enter purchase requisitions yourself or they can be generated automatically by the material planning and control system.

2. **Source Determination :-**
   The purchasing component helps us to identify potential sources of supply based on the past orders and existing longer term purchase agreements. This speeds the process of creating requests of quotation (RFQ) this can be sent to vendors electronically via SAP EDI (Electronic Data Interchange) if desired.

3. **Vendor Selection and Comparison of Quotation:**
   The system is capable of simulating pricing scenarios allowing us to compare a number of different quotations. Rejection letter can be sent automatically.

4. **Purchasing Order Processing:**
   The purchasing system adopts information from the requisition and the quotation to help you create a purchase order. As with purchase requisition, we can generate PO manually or have the system generate them automatically. Vendor scheduling agreements and contracts are also supported.

5. **Purchase Order Follow up:**
   The system checks the reminder periods that we specify and if necessary automatically prints reminders on expedites at the predefined intervals. It also provides you with an up-to-date status of all purchase requisitions, quotations, and purchase orders.

6. **Goods Receiving and Inventory Management:**
   Goods receiving personnel can confirm the receipt of goods simply by entering the PO number. By specifying permissible tolerances buyers can limit over- and under deliveries of ordered goods.

7. **Invoice Verification:**
   The system supports the checking and matching of invoice. The accounts clerk is notified of quantity and price variances because the system accounts clerk is notified of quantity and price variances because the system has access to PO and goods receipt data. This speeds the process of auditing and clearing invoices for payment

CPSIA information can be obtained at www.ICGtesting.com
Printed in the USA
LVOW09s1311250515

439683LV00004B/98/P